ECONOMICS OF PUBLIC CHOICE

Symposia on World and National
Issues—A Series

ECONOMICS OF
PUBLIC CHOICE

ROBERT D. LEITER
GERALD SIRKIN

EDITORS

Annual Volume of the Department of Economics, The City
College of the City University of New York

VOLUME II

Library of Congress Catalog Card Number 75–18626

ISBN 0–915326–02–7

MANUFACTURED IN THE UNITED STATES OF AMERICA

Preface

On May 16, 1974, the Economics Department of The City College of the City University of New York held its second annual conference. Seven papers, followed by seven comments, were delivered on the topic of "Economics of Public Choice." These papers and comments are published in this volume, along with an eighth manuscript prepared by Roger A. McCain which was submitted to the Department before the conference.

This publication has been made possible by income from the Harry Schwager Fund. All of our departmental colleagues have been generous when called upon to read and evaluate manuscripts submitted. Professor Morris Silver, chairman of the Department, was helpful at all stages of the project.

ROBERT D. LEITER

GERALD SIRKIN

The City College of the City University of New York

Contents

A Brief Background of
Public Choice Economics

ROBERT D. LEITER[*]

The economics of public choice, narrowly defined, deals with the many aspects of how economic resources are allocated by the political processes of government. More broadly, however, it encompasses all decision-making, whether public or private, that does not involve the conventional type of market analysis.

From the time of Adam Smith, economists have focused attention primarily on the subject of determining how limited resources are apportioned to alternative uses in the private sector through the operation of markets. Entrepreneurs producing goods and services in these markets are striving to maximize profits; other sellers of inputs are trying to maximize income; and consumers are attempting to maximize utility. It was clearly evident to Adam Smith and to economists who followed him that considerable economic activity took place outside the scope of profit-dominated markets. Examples include government activities relating to education, defense, administration of justice, interplanetary space, and pollution. Almost all government production and some private output involve welfare considerations and other nonprofit motives. Nevertheless, these areas were given little consideration in the mainstream of economic literature because they represented a small fraction of economic activity in the context of a laissez-faire capitalistic system.

* Professor of Economics, The City College of the City University of New York.

9

During the nineteenth and early twentieth centuries some economists did concern themselves with government planning in socialist economies, collective decision-making in capitalistic economies, and economic activity of nonprofit firms. It was recognized that public expenditures may involve moving resources from the private sector to the public sector and transferring income from some consumers to others. It was also clear that government intervention could alter allocation in the private sector through regulations, price controls, antitrust activities, and quotas. But historically, discussions of these factors were relatively uncommon in the standard works. Only in the past few decades have a growing number of economists turned their attention in a concerted and systematic way to an analysis of the role of government.

To a certain extent, economists have always been concerned with the theory of economic policy or welfare economics. In the twentieth century, however, greater attention has been directed by welfare economics to the effects of government policies and other economic occurrences on the desires of the public and the well-being of the community. The government's ability to adjust or compensate for departures from the competitive model resulting from monopolies, externalities, decreasing-cost production, and availability of public goods has been investigated and the relationship between public resource allocation and income redistribution has been explored. Such work by precursors of public choice economists has been done by Knut Wicksell, Arthur C. Pigou, Paul A. Samuelson, and William J. Baumol, among others.

Students of public choice economics depart from the classical approach of political scientists who deal with political decision-making in terms of power; instead, they use economic models (that is, choice theory), and even attempt quantification to explain the political process and solve political problems. Cost and benefit analysis, utility theory, and game theory applications were some of the devices first developed to understand the market place that are now used to analyze the political system and the role of government. Wilhelm von Humboldt, a political scientist, was among the first to compare the costs and benefits of government action in relation to external effects in *The Sphere and Duties of Government*, written near the beginning of the nineteenth century.

The leading students in the field of public choice today have broken new ground and moved into new areas. Their predecessors concentrated on the defects of the market system and generally felt that the problems arising from those defects could be solved by calling in the government. No questions were asked about how the government would do this work. But the currently important considerations and problems of public choice involve the ways in which non-market decisions are made, the defects in government decision-making, and the possibilities of improving the decision-making process. James M. Buchanan and Gordon Tullock gave some of the earliest impetus to the development of present-day studies of public choice.

Public choice examines the areas bearing on political decision-making to determine whether the policies and decisions of the executive and legislative branches of government are consonant with the will of the public. Some of the important matters studied include a search for a meaningful way of effecting majority rule through the election process; principles affecting individual citizens which underlie the functioning of a democratic society; and the interaction of political parties and political candidates with the politicians who mold them.

Certain similarities exist in the way in which the economic process and the political process satisfy the wants of the public. But costs and utility are balanced differently in the economic market and in the political system by consumers of goods and services. Consumer wants in the market become available through a procedure in which production is directly influenced by individual expenditures (a form of voting by spending). The government provides goods and services directly through its budget, but also establishes policies and enacts legislation that increase or decrease the purchasing power of individuals. Goods flowing from the political process are made available through the work of executives and legislators who normally cannot satisfy the conflicting majority and minority demands of citizens on many issues. Furthermore, unlike consumers who generally can limit purchases entirely to items they want, voters are rarely in agreement with all aspects of policy of candidates they vote for, yet must decide for a particular candidate at election time. These considerations markedly differentiate the processes by which the economic and political systems make goods and services available.

Public choice economics is also concerned with the subject of charity and charitable contributions because the conventional market generally does not function in this area. In both the private and the public sectors many nonexchange transactions occur. Individuals, business organizations, foundations, and governments are involved in unilateral transfers domestically and internationally, sometimes referred to as grants economics. The impact of charity on comparative production and productivity is investigated.

In general, the attention given to the role of government and public choice questions has been expanding greatly in the second half of the twentieth century. Especially during the decade of the 1970's, when inflationary forces are pushing prices inexorably upward, some economists minimize market forces when seeking explanations for the inability of the system to exercise moderation and control, and emphasize the importance of political decision-making. Impersonal market pressures are no longer paramount, but domestic politics, international relations, military leaders, and numerous ideologies are assigned responsibility for the course of economic events. A few economists who have expressed these notions, although they have made little analytical contribution to understanding the problems of public choice, include George Shultz, Kermit Gordon, and Robert Heilbroner. Thus the difficulties of dealing with inflation are political, in the view of some. Recently, professional economists have been wary of economic predictions because of the strong belief that economic events and the course of the economy are more subject to the effects of political decision-making. Public choice economics is slowly moving toward center stage as more analysis of government actions takes place.

In 1966, an economic journal entitled *Papers on Nonmarket Decision Making* was established. Two years later its name was changed to *Public Choice.* It offers the prime forum for articles in the field of public decision-making and from time to time has published extensive bibliographies of relevant materials.

The articles in this volume involve diverse aspects of public choice, but each discusses an important area of public policy. The first three authors present normative studies, dealing with what ought to be. Gerald Sirkin tells us that the causes of public choice failure are inherent in the system. Donald Wittman considers political decision-making and the strategy of political candidates. Dennis C. Mueller, Robert D. Tollison, and Thomas D. Willett propose a method of voting by the public which they suggest will appropriately reflect the intensity of feeling on issues that are being decided.

The remaining five studies are essentially positive, describing several matters of current interest. Roger A. McCain focuses on the theory of anarchy, finding that some norms and hypotheses of social choice are implicit in the ideas of the collectivist anarchists. Gordon Tullock presents an interesting analysis of the costs and benefits of investment for the purpose of improving the accuracy of information available in court trials. Morris Silver has written the only empirically oriented study in this volume, examining the hypothesis that preference for democracy is a function of income. Mancur Olson contradicts a generally accepted notion that conflict arises because of differences in the preferences of people. Finally, Richard D. Auster attempts to delineate the type of person attracted to public service, and considers whether recruits for government employment generally tend to be those who seek to avoid work or those who wish to avoid risk.

Each article is followed by cogent and interesting analysis. In a number of cases, the comments reflect sharp disagreement with the thesis of the article.

1

The Anatomy of Public Choice Failure

Gerald Sirkin*

The causes of the failure to optimize in a system of private choice has been reduced to a set of bare bones, systematically arranged, in Bator's "The Anatomy of Market Failure."[1] It appears premature to attempt, in a field so young as the analysis of public choice, what has been done in a field so old and intensively cultivated as the critique of the market system. But while the means are still limited, the need is great, for the discussion of economic policy continues to be carried on with apparent unawareness, even among many economists, that the inherent sources of failure in private choice have their counterpart in public choice.

By failure, I mean the failure to reach a Pareto optimum. The evidence of this failure stands out clearly in a variety of legislative actions. One can point to the continuation of obsolete military facilities to satisfy local interests; "pork barrel" construction for the same purpose; regulations to restrict entry into certain professions, crafts or businesses; resale price-maintenance laws; ceilings on interest rates; the failure to curtail unsightly roadside advertising; most restrictions on international trade; the agricultural price-support programs; and many other types of special-interest legislation. Such examples are only the tip of the iceberg that shows—the cases that most analysts could agree on. The bulk of the failures would be more difficult to demonstrate

* Professor of Economics, The City College of the City University of New York.

conclusively, but we suspect their presence from the evidence we have.

The discussion that follows is not concerned with all of the failures of the public sector, but only with the failures in making public choices. The *implementation* of these choices, involving problems of public administration and the nature of bureaucracy, is a separate area, replete with its own inherent sources of failure. Insofar as the bureaucracy affects the making of policy through its control of information and misinformation, it plays a part in the public choice process, but matters of implementation *per se* lie outside the scope of this paper.

I. CONDITIONS FOR OPTIMUM PUBLIC CHOICE

Analysis of market failure has been facilitated by the technique of specifying a theoretical model for reaching a Pareto optimum and then examining the divergences of actual systems from the model. The same technique should prove equally enlightening in the case of public choice.[2]

A.   The Choice Mechanism

1. *Democratic Process.* A democratic process of some sort is a minimum condition in this optimizing model, because the model is based on the individualistic postulate, i.e., that public choice is to be derived from individual preferences and the results are to be evaluated (as the Pareto criterion implies) by the standard of satisfying individual preferences. Without a democratic process (voting procedure), the model would have neither a method by which individual preferences could be known nor any assurance that they would be heeded.

2. *Voting Method.* The voting method must be one which assures a Pareto-optimal outcome. There are two possibilities.

(a) The Unanimity Rule

The requirement of unanimous agreement on public choices will, as Buchanan and Tullock have shown,[3] result in a Pareto-optimal outcome if the cost of reaching agreement is omitted. However, the Unanimity Rule must be rejected as a feasible voting method for at least the following reasons:

(1) The costs of reaching unanimous agreement, or any level approaching unanimity, will be extreme. Weighing the expected external costs of collective decisions against the costs of reaching agreement, each as a function of the proportion of voters required for agreement, voters will prefer a decision rule short of unanimity.[4]

(2) The distributional consequences of a unanimity rule will be perverse. Individuals will differ in their desire to reach an agreement. Those with the least interest, those with the least stake in the benefits to be derived from social cooperation, can bargain for the largest share of the benefits, since they have little or nothing to lose if no agreement is reached. In effect, the distribution will be biased in favor of those with the smallest marginal utility.

(3) A system based on a decision rule approaching unanimity will be unstable. A small number who believe they can improve their position under a rule requiring a lower proportion of acquiescent voters, or whose dominant preference is for anarchy, can, by withholding agreement, force a change in the decision rule.

(b) Vote Trading

A majority-rule system under which the set of public issues are decided simultaneously and under which each voter can exchange his votes on some issues for votes on other issues will bring the outcome closer to a Pareto optimum than a voting system without trading.

The success of the trading mechanism depends first, on the underlying structure of individual preferences. We can imagine a voting population polarized into two groups, of which one is a majority whose members all agree on the passage of certain measures and the rejection of others. In such circumstances (under a majority rule) no trading would take place. However, given sufficient dispersion of preferences, so that every voter holds some votes which have exchange value, the possibility of an improvement through vote trading exists.

The success of vote trading depends, secondly, on the trading arrangements. Optimum results from trading would require the following conditions:

(1) Vote exchange must not merely be agreed upon but must actually take place. Mere agreements to vote in a particular way cannot be enforced.[5]

(2) The number of buyers and sellers must be large enough to preclude monopoly or monopsony power through collusion.[6]

(3) All public issues must be decided simultaneously. Votes on each issue must be available for exchange on all other issues. If the total issues are divided into a number of separate bundles or if, after a vote, some issues are reintroduced for reconsideration, a less efficient outcome will result.

(4) As a corollary to the previous requirement, the opportunity to introduce proposals for public decision must be equally available to all individuals. Any bias in the introduction of proposals will reduce the efficiency of the system.

(5) Each voter, in making his trades, must allow correctly for the vote trading that will be done by other voters. The distribution of votes held by other voters will affect the probability that he can affect the outcome with his own votes, and will thereby affect the terms on which it will be advantageous for him to exchange votes.[7]

Vote trading, even with these conditions fulfilled, will not guarantee a Pareto optimum, but it will bring the outcome much closer to it than would a system of majority rule on each issue separately.[8]

However, in comparing public-choice mechanisms, the operating costs must be taken into account. The incremental costs of an improvement may exceed the incremental benefits. In the case of a vote-trading system, it may be that, with efficient markets, the costs of carrying out the exchanges will not be significant. But the costs in terms of *time* may be high. Existing public-choice systems entail high time cost; not only is anticipatory action generally impossible, but long lags are frequently experienced in adjusting public policy to changed conditions. It is to be expected that vote trading under the requirements outlined above will extend the lags, since decisions would have to wait upon the reopening and debate of the whole menu of public issues.

B. Voter Behavior

(1) Each voter must become correctly informed about the costs and benefits to himself from each issue.

(2) Voters (or an unbiased sample of voters) must trade votes in an effort to maximize expected utility, and actually cast their votes, even though the costs of these activities may exceed the expected gains.

II. DEVIATIONS FROM THE IDEAL

Democratic systems may contain elements of imposed public decisions. At the present time, in the U.S., we find the judiciary, which is not directly accountable to the electorate, imposing policies of its own choosing. Bureaucrats, through the looseness of administrative law, can impose policies of their own choosing. However, if the power to curb the judiciary and the bureaucracy is eventually in the hands of the electorate, then these departures from democratic process can be regarded as transitory.

A. The Choice Mechanism

The unanimity rule is nowhere applied, and in fact, the minimum proportion—the majority—is virtually the universal decision rule.

Vote trading is also not used. However, a rough variant—logrolling—ordinarily emerges in a democratic system. Analysis of the outcome of logrolling is extremely complex because of the variety of possible assumptions about the arrangements under which the logrolling is conducted.[9]

Whatever the arrangements assumed, logrolling can, at best, be only a crude substitute for the vote-trading requirements set out above. Consider the predominant system of voting for representatives, rather than voting directly on issues. Each representative is a log rolled into place by a coalition of voters with differing interests. As such, he is expected to collaborate with other representatives to roll into place a set of public decisions which will come as close as possible to the set he was elected to achieve. This logrolling procedure is inferior to the ideal vote-trading procedure in at least the following respects:

(1) Each candidate can stand for only one bundle of choices. Voters have a choice among only a small number of bundles. They have no means, through voting, of expressing their degree of preference for bundles not being offered. (It may be said that, in choosing his bundle, each candidate will have considered a large number of alternative bundles, seeking

the one which, in competition with the bundles of his opponents, has the greatest probability of attracting a majority of votes. If so, it could then be said that voters' preferences among a great number of possible bundles were taken into account. But, in the absence of any mechanism for voters to indicate the intensity of their preferences, candidates will lack the information necessary to do more than grope among a few alternatives.)

(2) Logrolling does not produce one bundle of all possible public choices. It proceeds by wrapping up a large number of separate bundles. Voters (through their representatives) do not have the opportunity of trading among all issues.

(3) Logrolling by representatives means exchanges by a small number of traders, which permits the exercise of monopoly or monopsony power.

It may be asked whether logrolling makes public choice more or less efficient. On the one hand, by allowing some trade-off among issues, it introduces some expression of intensity of preferences, and this improves the efficiency of the choice process. On the other hand, it increases the amount of "special-interest" legislation which is passed. A number of special-interest proposals, each of which would be defeated if voted on separately (with perfect information), may secure a majority as a bundle.

However, the fact that a proposal benefits a special interest does not, *per se*, establish it as inefficient. The net benefits to the gainers may exceed the costs to the losers. The inefficient proposals are those that yield a net total loss.

To examine whether logrolling leads to the adoption of inefficient proposals, consider the logrolling process carried to an organizational extreme. Assume that voters, with perfect information, are to choose one bundle of public policies from the set of all possible bundles of policies. The voting process would have to be complicated, possibly a preferential ranking system. But in the end, the bundle chosen would have to be Pareto optimal because, otherwise, it would always be possible to choose another bundle which would offer someone a gain, with no loss to the rest.

If, therefore, logrolling results in inefficient outcomes, it is not the logrolling itself, but the way in which it is carried out that produces that result. Voters are not offered a choice of one bundle among all possible bundles. Proposals are packaged in a number of bundles, each put together to secure a majority. If the majority is attained, no opportunity is offered to search for a superior bundle. In other words, logrolling is a crude and inefficient version of the complete vote-trading system.

B. Voter Behavior

It is possible that the failure of all voters to vote and a bias in the sample that does vote affects the optimality of the outcome. But I am unable to say anything about the actualities.

A more obvious and important problem concerns information. The requirement that each voter know the costs and benefits to himself from each proposal encounters two major obstacles.

The first obstacle is that investment in information for the purpose of voting does not pay. Even if the cost of information were modest, the return (expected benefit from the outcome of the voting multiplied by the likelihood that his vote will make a difference and adjusted for his estimate of the accuracy of his judgment) will almost always be smaller, leaving a negative pay-off.[10] And, of course, the cost of becoming informed on the great number of public issues is not modest. In fact, for most voters on most issues, the cost is infinite in the sense that, given the extremely limited capacity of the human mind, an understanding of more than a small number of relatively simple issues is impossible.

Consequently, a strong bias is introduced into voter calculations. Voters are best informed on those few issues that most directly concern them; that is, the issues from which they expect substantial effects on themselves, and on which they obtain information at little cost. Voters are relatively uninformed on more remote issues. The direct beneficiaries of a proposal will know of its benefits. The bearers of the cost will ordinarily be uninformed, since costs tend to be widely distributed, obscure, and complicated to calculate. When, on each issue, the gainers fully estimate the gain, and the losers underestimate the loss, the final bundle of public choices cannot be Pareto optimal.

The second major obstacle is that public choice is a field which is particularly prone to the production of misinformation.[11] Politicians gain from obfuscation, dissimulation, and the suppression of information because imperfect information eases the task of putting together a winning coalition to secure election or the passage of legislation they favor. Bureaucrats, who control a vital source of information, gain from misinformation which will assist in the continuation and expansion of the programs they administer. Also, the spokesmen for every special interest have an obvious reason to disseminate misinformation.

The production of misinformation is not unique to the public sector. But there is a difference between the public and private sectors which affects the scale of the problem. The countervailing forces of exposure and penalty are much weaker in the public sector than in the private.[12] In the private sector, there are many participants who have a direct interest in detecting and exposing dishonesty. In the public sector, the same cost-benefit relation which makes it unrewarding to invest in information also makes it unrewarding to invest in the detection and exposure of misinformation. Moreover, while government agencies are paid to monitor the honesty of the private sector, no answer has yet been found to the question of who will watch the watchman.

III. CONCLUSIONS

Two categories of failure-generators in democratic processes of public choice have been identified: defects in the
voting mechanism and information bias. Neither of these
can be corrected.

The correction of the voting defect by a system of vote
trading would require that all public issues be put up for a
vote simultaneously. In order to decide on any one issue,
all issues would have to be reopened. Direct voting on issues
would be necessary; representative systems would not be
permissible. When the high costs of this system are taken
into account—the costs of trading and voting, and the costs
in terms of delaying decisions until all issues can be re-
decided—vote trading may produce no movement toward
optimality from the position under the existing system even
if the outcome exclusive of costs were optimal. There is,
moreover, no assurance that the result of vote trading (exclusive of costs) will be optimal, though there is a high
probability that it will be substantially closer to an optimum
than systems of majority rule, either with or without logrolling.

The information bias cannot be corrected because it would
be irrational for individuals to invest in information which
would significantly reduce the bias, and because it is rational
for the managers of the public sector (politicians and bureaucrats) to increase the quantity of misinformation.

The solution to the welfare losses in public choice is,
therefore, not to be found in devices to improve the process,
though marginal improvements are possible. Greater improvements may be achieved by a more discerning selection of
the issues assigned to public choice. A careful weighing of
the respective failures of public and private choice might
show the advisability of reassigning certain decisions to the
private sector.

NOTES

1. Francis M. Bator, "The Anatomy of Market Failure," *Quarterly Journal of Economics*, lxxii, No. 3 (Aug., 1958), pp. 351–79.

2. This approach has been advocated by James S. Coleman in these terms: ". . . just as a free market with pure competition can be conceived in economic exchange, and used in a theoretical model from which actual systems can be examined, a similar model of pure competition can be conceived in collective decisions. Although actual social systems deviate from this model, it can nevertheless serve as a basis from which the deviations can be studied" ("The Possibility of a Social Welfare Function," *American Economic Review*, lvi, Dec., 1966).

3. James M. Buchanan and Gordon Tullock, *The Calculus of Consent*. Ann Arbor: Univ. of Michigan Press, 1962.

4. *Ibid.*, Chap. 6.

5. Dennis C. Mueller, "The Possibility of a Social Welfare Function: Comment," *American Economic Review*, lvii, No. 5 (Dec., 1967).

6. *Ibid.*

7. When the number of voters is very large, the probability of one voter's being able to affect the outcome of any issue, even after trading, will be insignificant. The need for information on other voters' trading then disappears, but is replaced by another problem. We are confronted with the question of why a voter will bother to trade, when the probability of affecting the outcome is insignificant. This question is similar to the question of why a voter incurs the cost of voting at all. (See Anthony Downs, *The Economic Theory of Democracy*; Gordon Tullock, *Toward a Mathematics of Politics*, Ann Arbor: Univ. of Michigan Press, 1967, Chap. VII. Yoram Barzel and Eugene Silberberg, "Is the Act of Voting Rational?" *Public Choice*, xvi [Fall, 1973]. Morris Silver, "A Demand Analysis of Voting Costs and Voting Participation," *Social Science Research*, Vol. 2, No. 2 [Aug., 1973].) For whatever reason he votes, which will presumably be for some psychic satisfaction rather than the expectation of affecting the outcome, he will trade votes for the same reason. The probability of affecting the outcome will be irrelevant to his trading, and consequently, the trades made by other voters will also be irrelevant.

8. See Dennis C. Mueller, Geoffrey C. Philpotts and Jaroslev Vanek, "The Social Gains from Exchanging Votes: A Simulation Approach," *Public Choice*, xii (Fall, 1972), in which the results suggest that the average outcome would be very close to the maximum potential utility. However, this outcome depends on the equal-stakes assumption, i.e., every voter was assumed to have the same total expected utility gain.

9. See, for example, Gordon Tullock, "Problems of Majority Voting," *Journal of Political Economy*, lxvii (Dec., 1959): 571-79; An-

thony Downs, "In Defense of Majority Voting," *Journal of Political Economy*, lxix (April, 1961): 192-99; Gordon Tullock, "Reply to a Traditionalist," *Ibid.*: 200-203.

10. See Gordon Tullock, *Toward a Mathematics of Politics*. Ann Arbor: Univ. of Michigan Press, 1967, Chap. VII.

11. *Ibid.*, Chap. IX.

12. See George T. Stigler, "The Economics of Conflict of Interest," *Journal of Political Economy*, 75, No. 1 (Feb., 1967).

Comments on
"The Anatomy of Public Choice Failure"

MALCOLM GALATIN[*]

There are a few brief comments I would like to make on Gerald Sirkin's paper. I would like to preface my remarks by stating that I find it very difficult to discuss problems of efficiency or optimality without a clear model of what is to be optimized.

First, I would question the usefulness of Pareto optimality as a criterion for measuring the success of a public-choice system. It seems to me that public choice is more concerned with movements along the contract (conflict) curve, i.e., how choices between Pareto optimal points are to be made, than about movements to the contract curve. Concentration on Pareto optimality leaves out of account the more interesting questions concerning the efficiency of a public-choice system.

Second, there are many interconnections between the systems of public and private choices. For example, if a particular industry requires workers with particular skills, the education of such workers may be raised as an issue in the public-choice system. Likewise, the provision of specific education for such workers, as an outcome of public choice, will affect the relative prices of goods and services in the private-choice system. In general, the private-choice system—the market system—functions under a number of

[*] Associate Professor of Economics, The City College of the City University of New York.

constraints imposed through the public-choice system, and the issues raised, and the mechanism of the public-choice system, are affected by the outcomes of the market system. Thus any discussion of the efficiency of one system should take into account its effect on the efficiency of the other. The interconnections between the systems of private and public choice must be examined in a more complete model if a really useful discussion of the efficiency of the public-choice system is to be attempted.

2

Political Decision-Making

DONALD WITTMAN[*]

Many authors, most notably Anthony Downs, have assumed that political candidates are only interested in winning the election.[1] In a single-peaked world with two candidates, the assumption implies that both will take a position close to the preferences of the median voter. This is an application of the "invisible hand" to politics and, just as in the economics of Adam Smith, competition and selfishness are shown to lead to an optimal situation—governmental representation of the majority position.

Unfortunately, this optimistic view does not coincide with some scholars' assessment that the political system is not responsive to the electorate. In an effort to reconcile some of these differing views I present an alternative assumption concerning candidate motivation—that they are solely interested in policy and that winning the election is just a means to that end. This assumption is shown to resolve a number of problems inherent in Downs' approach and to generate other interesting results.

There is considerable empirical evidence to suggest that policy issues are of prime concern to politicians. For example, in the 1964 U.S. Presidential election, the Republicans could have found someone besides Barry Goldwater with a better chance of winning the election. As another example,

---

[*] Assistant Professor of Economics, University of California at Santa Cruz.

in the postwar years the majority of people in Germany, France and Norway were overwhelmingly in favor of a neutralist foreign policy, yet their governments decided to join NATO.[2] More important evidence is found in the behavior of the incumbent. Kenneth Prewitt's interviews with local office holders (1969) found that they were often willing to go against the majority even at the risk of defeat. And certainly, the incumbent who is legally barred from being re-elected (e.g., a second-term president) does not have re-election as his ultimate goal. The point is not that the incumbent is unconcerned about being re-elected; rather that winning is just a means to an end. Thus the incumbent might implement policies which reduce his chances for re-election if the resulting increase in utility outweighs [the increased probability of losing the next election] times [the decreased utility if the opposition were to win and implement its policies].

This view resembles the theory of the firm, which assumes that the entrepreneur wants to maximize profits. Winning the election is a means to policy, just as selling goods is a means to profit. In contrast, the assumption that the candidate's goal is to win the election (maximize votes) is similar to the assumption that the firm wants to maximize sales.

A more realistic assumption is rarely a sufficient condition for accepting one approach and rejecting another; it is also necessary for the assumption to yield results which are more interesting and predictive. In the following sections, I will attempt to show that these conditions hold when it is assumed that the candidates are interested in implementing policy. In addition, I will extend and correct some of the results of Downs' model. Both approaches will be compared in a variety of situations—the simple examples giving insights into the essential concepts and the more complex cases presenting a closer approximation to reality.

I. SINGLE-PEAKEDNESS WITH PERFECT INFORMATION

In this section it is assumed that a left-right continuum exists such that every individual's utility is a single-peaked function of that continuum and there is perfect information (i.e., *both candidates know all the individuals' utility functions, and given any two choices each individual will always vote for that choice which gives him the most utility*; when the choices are identical, he votes for each with probability equal to 1/2). If each candidate wants to maximize the probability of winning the election, then the candidates would look alike, each presenting a platform close to the median voter's preferred position.[3] If either candidate did otherwise, he would have a lower probability of winning the election. For example, if one candidate took a position to the left while the other candidate remained at the median voter's favored position, then the median voter and all the voters to his right would vote for the right candidate. Therefore the left candidate would lose with probability equal to 1.

Under the assumption of policy as the goal, the candidates will also look alike, yet their platforms need not be at the favored position of the median voter. For example, even if almost all the voters' preferred positions are on the left, neither candidate will present a platform to the left of the left candidate's preferred position as both candidates would have greater utility if the left-most candidate moved right, since utility depends on which policy is implemented, not on winning *per se*.[4] Thus if the candidates are concerned with policy issues, they may not be responsive to the interests of the voters. On the other hand, if the median voter's preferred position is between those of the candidates, then each candidate will choose his platform to coincide with the median voter's preference (in this case the results are similar to Downs). To illustrate, both candidates would not be to the left of the median voter for it would always pay the candidate whose preferred position was to the right to move right, as both the probability and utility of his winning would increase. Nor would the candidate whose preferred position was to the left be to the left and the candidate whose preferred position was to the right be to the right of the median voter. If a candidate has zero chance of winning he could always increase his expected utility by moving closer to the median voter. And if both candidates had some probability of winning, then either could move infinitesimally closer to the median voter and improve his expected utility, as the candidate would then win with certainty by making all the previously indifferent voters prefer him.

II. SINGLE-PEAKEDNESS WITH IMPERFECT INFORMATION

Voters often do not vote for the candidate which gives them the most utility. There are three reasons why they do not: 1) the voter wants to threaten his favored candidate so that if he does not alter his policy, the candidate will lose his vote in present and future elections, and therefore the voter abstains; 2) the voter realizes that the cost involved in voting (time lost, etc.) is greater than the probability of his vote affecting the outcome times the additional utility derived from the change in outcome, and therefore he abstains; and 3) the voter is uninformed and therefore votes for the wrong candidate.

Almost all the modeling of candidate behavior has assumed vote or plurality maximization. With perfect information the results are identical to the assumption of maximizing the probability of winning. However, with imperfect information they are not equivalent. For example, a candidate who maximizes the probability of winning would prefer to have 51 percent of the voters vote for him with 100 percent probability and 49 percent of the voters vote for him with probability 0, than to have 100 percent of the voters vote for him with 55 percent probability. The plurality or vote maximizing candidate would have a reverse order of preference. In the following analysis, I will assume that each candidate maximizes the probability of being elected and that voters may mistakenly vote for the wrong party. Surprisingly, these have not been dealt with by Downs or Hinnich and Ordershook (who only deal with abstention and with maximization of votes or plurality).[5]

A. Effect of Imperfect Information on Candidate Position

Although the rationality of threatening abstention has been argued (for example, by Downs who assumes vote maximization), in fact such behavior is irrational when the candidates want to maximize the probability of being elected. This can be seen in Figure 1. In situation A there is perfect information and neither candidate will move either to the left or to the right away from the median voter. In B some of the left have become more extreme and have threatened to boycott the election. Neither candidate will move left because even if all the extremists were willing to vote for him, the candidate would be in a minority position. In fact, both candidates move to the right and are at the most preferred position of the median voter of those actually voting. In C the right threatens also, which shifts the candidates back to the left.[6] The same results hold true when the voter abstains because the costs of voting are too high.

The effect of the uninformed voter is virtually the same as that of the abstainer. The abstainer threatens the candidate with a one-vote loss. He could also threaten to vote for the other candidate. The original candidate would then risk losing two votes, and consequently the abstainer and the uninformed voter look alike to the candidates. That is, their motivations are different, but their actions are similar—not always voting for the candidate which gives them the most

FIGURE 1

If the candidates are only interested in winning the election
and the world is single-peaked, then both candidates will be
at the median voter's most preferred position.

B

A

Abstention by left
No abstention

Left extremist threaten not to
vote if difference is small

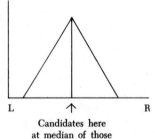

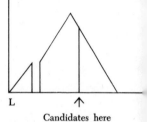

Number of
voters
voting

L   ↑   R

Candidates here
at median of those
voters voting

L   ↑

Candidates here
at median of those
voters voting

C

Abstention by right in
addition to abstention by left

Right extremist also threaten
not to vote

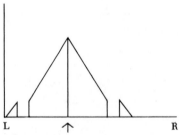

L   ↑   R

Candidates here
at median of those
voters voting

"Rational abstention" will cause the candidates to move
in the opposite direction.

utility. Therefore, just like the abstainer the uninformed voter will move the candidate in the opposite direction.

Threatening to vote perversely (i.e., to have a greater than 50 percent chance of voting for the candidate whose position is either farther away or identical to the other candidate's position) may be rational. For instance, if the voters on the left threaten to vote for the right candidate unless the left candidate moves left to position L and the left candidate does not heed this warning, then, even if the parties look alike, the probability of the left candidate winning will be less than 50 percent because all the voters except the left will be indifferent between the two candidates. If this probability is less than the probability of the candidate winning when he takes position L, then the candidate will move left to L.

If the candidates are only interested in winning the election, they will not become less similar because the voters are uninformed (unless they vote perversely).[7] It must benefit one of the two candidates to look more like the other. If it increases the left candidate's probability of winning to move left in order to look less like the opposition, it must benefit the right candidate to also move left so that he will still look like the left candidate. In short, one candidate can always assure himself of a 50 percent chance of victory by resembling the other candidate.[8] If the distribution of uninformed voters and abstainers is symmetric around the median voter, then an equilibrium will exist if both parties choose a position close to that of the median voter.[9] The reasoning is as follows:

Assume that the opposition does not choose the median position and instead takes a position to the left. Voters to the left of the opposition are more likely to vote for him since he no longer resembles the incumbent; however, to the majority this clear differentiation favors the incumbent. Therefore he will place himself at the median voter's preferred position. If the voters on the left are better informed than those on the right, both candidates will move to the left, again looking alike.

When the candidates are interested in policy, the easiest way to understand what transpires is to begin where we left off—with both candidates having the same platform. Let the left candidate have his preferred platform to the left and the right candidate his preferred platform to the right of the actual position that both have chosen. The left candidate is willing to move left, even though this reduces the probability of winning, because when he wins, the win is worth more. However, he will not move further left than his favored position as this decreases the probability that he will win, and if he wins, the utility that the candidate receives is less. The same holds true for the right candidate. As shown earlier, when the voters have perfect information, the candidates will look just alike. If the voters are totally uninformed, then whichever position a candidate chooses will have a 50 percent chance of winning the election. Consequently each candidate will present its preferred platform. As the voters become more informed, both candidates will take into account the chance of their platform winning and the candidates will become more similar. It should be noticed that a candidate's expected utility depends on the probability of his winning times the utility of his platform being enacted plus the probability of his losing times the utility (or disutility) he derives from his opponent's position being enacted.

B. Plurality vs. Coalition Governments

In a plurality system where candidates are only interested in policy there will be a tendency for only two candidates to exist, for if there are three candidates the extreme left (or extreme right) is taking away votes from the middle candidate and thereby increasing the probability that the right-most (left-most) candidate will win. Thus, the existence of two candidates to the left of the median voter tends to be counter-productive to the two left candidates. In contrast, where majority votes are required (coalition governments) the number of candidates increases. Here a new left candidate is not counter-productive since he may increase the total number of votes on the left by picking up voters who previously abstained. The same logic does not apply to candidates that are only interested in winning, for then it is not counter-productive in a plurality system for a new candidate to exist. Consequently, Downs' model would deny that there would be more candidates when there are coalition governments; yet this is in fact the case.[10]

III.   DECISION-MAKING WITH INTRANSITIVITY

A.   Competition

Given the diverse interests of the electorate and the complexity of the issues, it is unlikely that the world is single-peaked. Therefore, in this section it will be assumed that the world is intransitive—i.e., *no one platform is preferred by a majority of voters to all the other platforms.*

If the candidates are solely interested in winning, then the set of possible choices is at best only restricted to the set of platforms on the cycle of intransitivity. The maximization of winning gives no guide, for whatever platform is chosen can be beaten. The existence of imperfect information only aggravates the problem, for different platforms may look just alike to the voters and thus have the same probability of winning.

If the candidates are interested in policy, then each may be able to rank the alternatives according to expected utility. For example, if the candidate has a choice of three platforms, A, B, or C, each having the same probability of winning, and in every case the opposition presents a fourth platform D, then the candidate will obviously choose that platform which he prefers. The analysis may be more complex. As mentioned before, expected utility also depends on the choice of platform the opposition chooses. It is quite possible that the candidate may structure the set of issues to force the opposition into presenting a platform which is acceptable to the candidate. To use a standard (if somewhat unrealistic) example from the literature; assume that the world is intransitive, there is perfect information and that the incumbent presents his platform first—this being a model of the usual situation where the incumbent implements policies to which the opposition either suggests alternatives or concurs.[11] The opposition will select the platform that, given the incumbent's choice and the preferences of all the individuals, will bring the most utility to the opposition—(provided that it is preferred by a majority to the incumbent's choice). Depending on the structure of preferences, it is possible that there is no platform which both gives the opposition greater utility than he would derive from the incumbent's platform and wins the election. In such a situation he would either present the same platform as the incumbent or present a losing one. The incumbent, realizing that the opposition will act in this way, examines the set of alternatives that the opposition will choose, given alternative platform choices by the incumbent, and selects that alternative which results in the most utility for himself. As an example, let the majority of voters prefer A to B, B to C, C to D, A to C, B to D, and D to A. Let the incumbent prefer C to D, D to B, and B to A; and let the opposition prefer A to B, B to C, and C to D. The incumbent would be most happy with C; however, he realizes that if he presented C, the opposition would present A—the incumbent's least preferred platform. A is the most preferred position of the opposition and is preferred by a majority of voters to C. The incumbent therefore presents D, his second most preferred platform. The opposition will choose B, which he and the majority of voters prefer to D. The opposition will not choose A as it would lose to D, and he will not choose C as he prefers B to C.

In general, the strategy of the incumbent is to force a set

of options on the opposition such that opposition a) prefers winning with a platform more beneficial to the incumbent rather than winning with one less beneficial to the incumbent and b) prefers a platform with a lower probability of winning rather than one with a higher probability of winning and which, if enacted, would cause serious disutility to the incumbent.[12] In other words, whenever possible the candidate tries to structure the situation so that the platform which creates serious disutility to himself would also create serious disutility to the opposition, and therefore the opposition will avoid these possibilities.

It should be remembered that voters tend to be extremely uninformed about politics and that candidates are often vague about their policies. In such situations there is considerable leeway for the victorious candidate and it is even possible for him to renege on his promises. With elections being such a weak market mechanism for revealing voter preferences, both because of poor information and intransitivity, it is not surprising that elected officials often choose their own preferred position on a policy issue. Certainly, for many issues the model of total ignorance and intransitivity by the voters is the most appropriate. In such cases, the winning candidate would implement his own most preferred policies. The more the voters are informed and the more they are of like mind, the more the politician must take into account the effect of his policies on being re-elected and the more his own personal desires will be tempered.

B. Collusion

If the candidates are only interested in winning the election, there can be no collusion, for the election is a zero-sum game.[13] In contrast, if the candidates are interested in policy, it is natural for them to collude.[14] For example, they might invoke "bipartisanship" if their views were similar but differed from the electorate. As another example, "fair play" or "belief in democracy" might prevent each candidate from suggesting policies which were truly damaging to the opposition. In this way certain issues would never become issues. This is an obvious analogy to restricted competition by oligopolists in the business world where there is greater competition in advertising than in price.

If the candidates have convex utility functions (in an election concerned with income distribution this would mean decreasing marginal utility of income), there would always be a sure thing preferred by both candidates to a gamble. Collusion would then result in the candidates looking alike and would be less risky than offering dissimilar platforms. Again the political candidates would not necessarily be responsive to the interests of the voters.

Unlike Downs' model, the voters cannot rely on competition between the candidates to produce an optimal choice. First of all, as shown in Section I, the choices presented by competing candidates may be way to the left (or right) of the majority voter. In the second place, the candidates may collude and not offer the voters a significant choice.

IV.   ELECTIONS CONCERNED WITH INCOME DISTRIBUTION

In this section I assume that the election is solely concerned with income distribution and that each voter's utility depends only on the amount of income that he receives. There are a number of reasons why I assume that the only issue is income distribution: 1) this is an intransitive situation (Ward 61); 2) the question of income distribution in particular is of great importance to every government; and 3) being a constant sum situation, this is an example of pure conflict and it is important to know what the results are in this general case.

A.   Abstention

If a voter either mistakenly or intentionally does not vote for the candidate which offers him the most (because the offerings are so similar), what effect does this have on the amount of income that he will be promised by the candidates? In general he will be offered less by both of them, since it is impossible to threaten both candidates at once. To threaten the opposition that you will not vote for it (i.e., increase the probability of the opposition losing) is to promise the incumbent that you will not vote against it (i.e., increase the likelihood of the incumbent winning) and the incumbent will take advantage of this promise by offering less (the result is analogous to the single-peaked case). However, if the incumbent is already offering nothing, he cannot offer less and in order for the opposition to keep your vote, he may offer you more. Of course, both candidates always have the option of offering nothing to any or all of the voters if the costs are too high. For example, if all of the voters are totally uninformed, then no matter how much more one candidate offers, the probability that he will win is unchanged. Therefore neither candidate will offer anything to the voters.

B. Loyalty and Preference

Imperfect information can take other forms. For example, a voter may feel party loyalty and vote for one candidate even if the other offers him more. The reasons are many: biased sources of information; peer group pressure; habit; a comparatively better policy in previous elections; etc. In order to study the effects of loyalty and preferences it will be useful to introduce the following concepts. *Let the amount of income that candidate* Y *offers a voter minus the amount that candidate* X *offers be the candidate income differential.* The greater the candidate income differential, the greater the probability that the voter will vote for Y. *A voter is said to be loyal to a candidate if the probability that he votes for him is greater than one-half when the candidate differential is zero.*[15] *A candidate is said to have a loyal numerical majority if the number of voters loyal to him is greater than the number loyal to the other candidate. A candidate is de-*

fined as having a loyal probabilistic majority if the probability of victory is greater than one-half when both candidates make equal offers. A candidate with a numerical majority need not have a probabilistic majority. For example, let Voter A vote for X with probability 1 and Voters B and C each vote for Y with probability 2/3. Then Y has a loyal majority but has a loyal probabilistic minority, for other things being equal, he would only win 4/9 of the time. This may explain why California, with a numerical majority of Democrats, so often votes Republican; the Republicans are more loyal than the Democrats.

The following will show that, other things being equal, neither candidate will offer income to those voters who prefer the party with a numerical minority.

Two voters are said to be equally sensitive to income differentials if the change in probability of each voter voting for a candidate with respect to a change in the income differential is equal and constant. That is, if two voters are equally sensitive to income differentials, then if Y increases his offer to each voter by the same amount, each voter will increase the probability of his voting for Y by the same amount whatever the initial offering by X and Y to each of the voters (see Figure 2).

A candidate is defined as having a numerical majority if a majority of voters prefers him. A numerical majority is not the same as a loyal numerical majority, since the candidate differential may be great enough to overcome the handicap of only having a loyal numerical minority.

If the voters have the same sensitivity to income differentials, then neither candidate will offer income to those voters who prefer the candidate with a numerical minority. The following is a heuristic proof (for a mathematical one see footnote 16). For any given amount of income that a candidate gives to the voters, he will seek to maximize the probability of his winning the election. The probability of the candidate with the numerical majority winning the elec-

FIGURE 2

No Candidate Loyalty, But Different Levels of Information

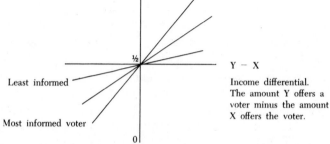

Probability of voting for Y

Candidate Loyalty, But All the Voters Are Equally
Sensitive to Income Differentials

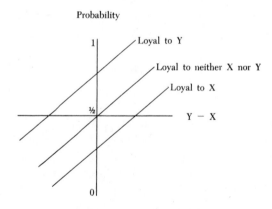

Probability

tion will be greater if he increases the probability of one of
those voters voting for him who prefers him, than of one who
prefers the minority candidate. When the voters are equally
sensitive to income differentials, it takes the same amount
of income to change the probability of an individual voting

for a candidate from 50% to 100% as it takes to change the probability of 50 individuals from 50% to 51%. For the same cost it is better for the majority candidate to insure that a majority of voters are very likely to vote for him than to have more voters who are each less likely to vote for him (e.g., the candidate is more likely to win if 51% of the voters vote for him with 100% probability and 49% with 0% probability than if 100% of the voters vote for him with 51% probability). Thus the majority candidate will only give income to those voters who prefer the majority candidate. The same logic holds for the minority candidate. He can best decrease the probability of the majority candidate winning by promising income to those voters who prefer the majority candidate.

This suggests why Barry Goldwater was bound to lose in the 1964 presidential election. He concentrated his campaign on the minority of voters who already were strongly in favor of his candidacy. He would have had a better chance of winning if he had tried to attract some of the voters who leaned towards Lyndon Johnson, for Goldwater began (and ended) the campaign with a numerical minority of voters preferring him.[17]

C. Advertising Versus Platform

Each candidate spends money on advertising and other forms of information in order to persuade individuals to vote for him. The likelihood that an individual votes for a candidate depends on both the candidate platform differential and the advertising differential, making it possible for a voter who is loyal to neither candidate to have a higher probability of voting for candidate X than candidate Y even though X has offered less than Y, if X has spent much more than Y on advertising. Of course the greater the platform differential, the harder it is for X to convince the voter that he has offered a larger amount.

There is a trade-off between advertising and platform. The more (less) a candidate offers, the less (more) he needs to advertise.[18] The more informed the voters are, the more responsive they are to platform differentials and the less responsive to other means of persuasion. Thus if the voters are perfectly informed, there is no need for the candidates to spend large amounts on advertising their differences (as they are already known). Conversely, the less informed the voters are, the more the candidates will spend on information and the less they will give the voters.

V. CONCLUSION

This paper has extended and reinterpreted some of the results of Downs' approach to political strategy and has introduced an alternative model which assumes that the candidates are only interested in policy and that winning the election is just a means to that end. The alternative model has proven to be very useful as it has produced a number of implications which differ from those of Downs—the most important of these being that the candidates tend to be insensitive to the interests of the voters.

At best, an election can only clarify the voters' attitudes on a very few issues, and even on these issues the majority viewpoint is not clearly delineated. This means the politician has little information regarding what the voters want. Combined with the fact that the voters have little information on what the incumbent did, it should not be surprising that the politicians refer to their own conscience (i.e., utility function) for judgment rather than the unknowable majority will.[19]

NOTES

1. Two variations on the theme are vote maximization and plurality maximation.

2. For example, in August 1951, 60 percent of the West German population "chose neutrality between Americans and Russia as the best policy for Germany" (K. Deutsch [1959], p. 23). It should also

be noted that politicians rarely pay attention to polls on issues and even more rarely take them. For other examples, see R. Hamilton (1971).

3. The word platform will be used interchangeably with position or policy choice and refers to a point in a policy space.

4. In this case the lower the barriers to entry, the more the candidates will move to the left. This is analogous to the situation in business where a monopoly may lower prices (temporarily) to drive out competitors. Lower barriers to entry obfuscate the results in the vote maximizing model even more, as no clear answer can be obtained. New parties could start on either side or between the existing parties. As shown in Section II B, starting a new party is not counter-productive to the new party if it is only interested in winning. Entry barriers in politics are probably extremely high. The government is a collective good and thus voting for a third party is counter-productive if it makes your second-best alternative lose to the third-best alternative. Thus, parties which receive few votes are not viable in a plurality system. This does not hold true in the business world. Even if no one else buys what you buy, you still consume the good. Finally, informing the voters of your policies and gaining their confidence takes considerable money and/or manpower.

5. B. Barry (1970) has argued this point.

6. Even if abstention by the left caused the left candidate to move left, this does not necessarily mean that abstention is rational. If the candidate moves left it will have a lower probability of winning than if it had remained in the same position and there was no abstention by the left voters. Consequently, those voters on the left may have a lower expected utility since their preferred position is less likely to win. Furthermore, the voters may have to proceed with their threat if the candidate does not move left. This lowers their utility from the present election, which is irrational unless the voters are future-oriented.

7. This is contrary to the work of Downs which claims that the threat of abstention keeps the candidates from looking alike. For a more mathematical treatment of this and several other propositions, see D. Wittman (1974).

8. The results are the same if one party is always considered the left party and the other party is always considered the right party even when their platforms are identical.

9. However, there may be many other equilibria, e.g., if all voters are totally uninformed, any two platforms (even if dissimilar) will be in an unstable equilibrium.

10. Most of Downs' results for three or more candidates do not hold together logically.

11. There are other variations. For example, it could be assumed that the incumbent must present the platform he ran on previously,

or that each party can only change its platform slightly; these complicate the analysis but do not change the essential results.

12. Depending on the particular structure of preferences and information it is still possible for intransitive situations to result when the candidates are interested in policy.

13. They might collude to reduce campaign expenses or to split offices.

14. It is not necessary to assume that the platforms are presented sequentially.

15. A more useful definition of loyalty is that a voter is loyal to Y if for all amounts x and y, the probability of the voter voting for Y when Y offers amount y and X offers amount x is greater than the probability of the voter voting for X when X offers amount y and Y offers amount x. The definition in the main body of the paper is broader than this one, but when it is combined with the other assumptions in the paragraph the resulting definition is narrower.

16. This can be shown mathematically. Assume that there are three voters 1, 2 and 3, who vote for Y with probability P_1, P_2 and P_3, respectively, with $P_1 < 1/2$ and $P_2, P_3 > 1/2$. Thus Y has a numerical majority. Y has a choice of increasing P_1 by $\delta > 0$ or P_3 by δ. If P_1 is increased by δ, then the probability that Y will win the election is

$$1) \quad [P_1 + \delta]\, P_2 P_3 + [P_1 + \delta]\, P_2\, [1 - P_3]$$
$$+ [P_1 + \delta]\, P_3\, [1 - P_2] + P_2 P_3\, [1 - P_1 - \delta]$$

$$2) \quad = P_1 P_2 P_3 + P_2 P_3 \delta + P_1 P_2 - P_1 P_2 P_3 + \delta P_2 - \delta P_2 P_3$$
$$+ P_1 P_3 - P_1 P_2 P_3 + \delta P_3 - \delta P_3 P_2 + P_2 P_3 - P_1 P_2 P_3 - \delta P_2 P_3$$

$$3) \quad = - 2P_1 P_2 P_3 + P_1 P_2 + P_1 P_3 + P_2 P_3 + \delta P_2 + \delta P_3 - 2\delta P_2 P_3$$

If P_3 is increased by δ, then the probability that Y will win the election is

$$4) \quad P_1 P_2\, [P_3 + \delta] + P_1 P_2\, [1 - P_3 - \delta] + P_1\, [P_3 + \delta]\, [1 - P_2]$$
$$+ P_2\, [P_3 + \delta]\, [1 - P_1]$$

$$5) \quad = P_1 P_2 P_3 + P_1 P_2 \delta + P_1 P_2 - P_1 P_2 P_3 - P_1 P_2 \delta + P_1 P_3$$
$$+ P_1 \delta - P_1 P_2 P_3 - P_1 P_2 \delta + P_2 P_3 - P_1 P_2 P_3 + P_2 \delta - P_1 P_2 \delta$$

$$6) \quad = - 2P_1 P_2 P_3 + P_1 P_2 + P_1 P_3 + P_2 P_3 + P_1 \delta - P_2 \delta - 2P_1 P_2 \delta$$

is $6 \overset{?}{>} 3$. Subtracting off elements in common,

$$7) \quad \delta\, [P_1 + P_2 - 2P_1 P_2] \overset{?}{>} \delta\, [P_2 + P_3 - 2P_2 P_3]$$

$$8) \quad = \delta\, [P_1 - 2P_1 P_2] \overset{?}{>} [P_3 - 2P_2 P_3]$$

$$9) \quad = \delta P_1\, [1 - 2P_2] \overset{?}{>} \delta P_3\, [1 - 2P_2]$$

$$10) \quad \text{Since } P_2 > 1/2,\ [1 - 2P_2] < 0,$$

11) $\delta P_1 [1 - 2P_2] > \delta P_3 [1 - 2P_2]$ as $P_1 < P_3$

Therefore Y will not increase the probability of Voter 1 who prefers the minority candidate. This being true, the reverse must also be true—the probability of the candidate with a numerical minority winning the election will be greater if it decreases the probability of voting for the majority candidate of one of those voters who prefer the majority candidate (than if it decreases the probability of voting for the majority candidate of one of those voters who prefer the minority candidate). Unlike the analysis in the rest of the paper neither candidate considers counter moves by the other.

17. Many claim that both candidates must appeal to their loyal voters as they are the ones who get out the vote. If this is true, then the voters are not equally as sensitive to income differentials. See A. Hirschman (1970) for a discussion of loyalty.

18. This is similar to the situation in economics: those brands that are heavily advertised generally have higher prices than those which are not, suggesting both that those candidates which spend more on campaigns may offer the voters less, and that minor candidates without funds will have to offer the voters more if they want to affect the outcome of the election. There may also be a trade-off between loyalty and advertising.

19. The candidate can always convince himself that what he wants coincides with the majority.

REFERENCES

1. Barry, Brian M. (1970). *Sociologists, Economists and Democracy.* London: Collier-Macmillan Limited.
2. Deutsch, Karl W. and Lewis J. Edinger (1959). *Germany Rejoins the Powers.* Stanford: Stanford University Press.
3. Downs, Anthony (1957). *An Economic Theory of Democracy.* New York: Harper and Bros.
4. Hamilton, Richard (1971). *Class and Politics in the United States.* New York: John Wiley.
5. Hinich, Melvin and Peter Ordershook. "Plurality Maximization vs. Vote Maximization: A Spatial Analysis with Variable Participation." *American Political Science Review,* 64 (September, 1970).
6. Hirschman, Albert O. (1970). *Exit, Voice and Loyalty.* Cambridge, Mass.: Harvard University Press.
7. Prewitt, Kenneth. "Political Ambitions, Volunteerism and Electoral Accountability." *American Political Science Review,* 64 (March, 1970).
8. Wittman, Donald (1974). *Equilibrium Strategies by Political Candidates.* Unpublished manuscript.
9. Wittman, Donald. "Parties as Utility Maximizers." *American Political Science Review,* LXVII, No. 2 (June, 1973).

Comments on
"Political Decision-Making"

GERALD SIRKIN[*]

The assumption in political analysis that politicians have only one objective—winning elections—is equivalent to the assumption in economic analysis that farmers are price takers and not price makers. There is no implication that farmers wouldn't *like* to make prices, but only that they can't. Similarly, if politicians are assumed to be policy takers, and not policy makers, it is implicitly being assumed, not that politicians wouldn't like to make policy, but that they can't. Their own preferences about policy are, in that case, irrelevant to the analysis. In order to introduce politicians' policy preferences into the analysis, one must show that the state of the market leaves room for those preferences to play a part. The first task facing Professor Wittman is to locate the room for politicians' policy preferences.

In his first case—single-peakedness with perfect information and two candidates—the situation is like the duopoly problem, in which the outcome depends on the decision rule of the duopolists. If each ignores the reaction of the other, each will attempt to ensure a victory by moving toward the position of the median voter, until both take identical positions at the median. If each takes into account the reactions of the other, then each will be aware that the highest probability of winning which he can hope for is 0.5. In that case, they can choose from among a number of posi-

---

* Professor of Economics, The City College of the City University of New York.

tions in which each has a 0.5 probability of winning. At this point, the candidates' policy preferences do have a bearing on their choice of positions. If the preferred positions of both are on the same side of the median, then, as Professor Wittman says, they will adopt identical positions at whichever of the preferred positions is closer to the median. But, if the candidate's preferred positions are on opposite sides of the median, then contrary to Professor Wittman's conclusion, they will not reach identical positions at the median. Whichever candidate's preference is closer (measured in number of voters) to the median can take his stand at his preferred position and the opponent can choose a position on his own side of the median, such that each will have a 0.5 probability of winning.

All of this reasoning, however, is based on the assumption of closed entry. If entry of other candidates is not blocked, then two candidates taking positions away from the median may create a highly attractive situation for a third candidate. If the first two candidates are on the same side of the median, any third candidate who takes a position closer to the median will believe he is certain of winning (if he ignores the reactions of the first two). The entry of the third candidate will force all three to move toward the median. If the first two candidates are on opposite sides of the median, a sufficient space between them will make a third candidate expect to obtain a plurality with a position at the median,[1] if he ignores the reactions of the original candidates. This threat will compel the candidates to draw closer to the median.

In the case of single-peakedness with imperfect information, a clearer distinction should have been made between the imperfection of the voters' information and the candidates' information. If the voters are imperfectly informed about where their best interests lie, but the candidates know exactly how the voters will vote, then the behavior of the candidates will be determined by the same principles as it would be if the voters were perfectly informed. But, if the candidates have imperfect information about how voters will vote, so that each policy position has some probability of winning, then it will be rational for each candidate to weigh, for each platform, both the probability of winning and the utility of that platform to himself. Professor Wittman has an interesting and insightful point here.

However, it seems to me that more should be added to Professor Wittman's formula. Winning an election and holding office yields utility for its own sake, apart from the policy achievements it may permit. Also, winning an election does not assure the politician that he can achieve his policy objectives. Hence, the formula should take account of the probability that either the candidate or his opponent can implement his policy. Thus, let

P_{wj} = probability of winning with policy j
P_{lj} = probability of losing with policy j
U_o = utility of being in office
U_j = utility of policy j to candidate A
U_k = utility (or disutility) of opponent's policy to Candidate A
P_a = probability that A can achieve policy
P_b = probability that A's opponent can achieve his policy
V_a = value of election to candidate A

Then,

$$V_a = P_{wj}(U_o + P_a U_j) + P_{lj}(P_b U_k)$$

If the probabilities of achieving policy (P_a and P_b) are small (as would likely the the case for any one politician in the American system), then the utility of policies becomes a small item in the calculation, and the probability of winning becomes the dominant term in the equation.

In the case of intransitivity, several forms of behavior can be considered, none of which seems to make much sense when related to real political behavior. If the candidates are assumed capable of constantly changing their positions before the election, then either repeated adjustments of positions will occur with victory going to the candidate who gets in the last word, or else they will both find it advisable to adopt the same position. If candidates must adhere to a position once announced, then victory goes to the candidate who makes the last announcement of his position. Professor Wittman visualizes one candidate taking his stand first and gallantly laying down his (political) life to force his opponent to win on the least objectionable platform. If that prediction does not match our ordinary conception of politicians, it may be because the intransitivity case is not realistic.

The hypothesis that the state of the voting market leaves significant room for politicians to pursue their own preferences has obviously important implications for the "representativeness" of representative governments. But I do not see any convincing empirical tests of the hypothesis. The fact that candidates sometimes take distinctly different positions is not necessarily evidence for the hypothesis. For example, we may predict that candidates will be either "look-alikes" or take distinctly different positions, even if the sole consideration is the probability of winning. In single-peak situations with perfect information, the candidates will reach identical or differing positions, depending on the decision rule they adopt. In single-peak situations with imperfect information, the candidates may take identical or differing positions, according to their own estimates of the most probable winning position.

Pending further empirical evidence and tests, we may do best to fall back on a deductive proposition: given a world of changing voters' preferences, political competition, and survival of the fittest, we should predict that politicians with strong policy attachments tend to be weeded out and the survivors will tend to be those with the single objective of winning.

NOTE

1. If the space between the first two candidates contains more than 2/3 of the votes, a third candidate at the median position can expect to get more than 1/3 of the votes.

3

Solving the Intensity Problem in Representative Democracy

DENNIS C. MUELLER, ROBERT D. TOLLISON,
AND THOMAS D. WILLETT*

The problem of the representation of minority interests under one man-one vote majority rule has never been satisfactorily resolved in democratic theory or in its application. The typical statement of the problem depicts the victory of a lethargic majority over an intense minority, to the detriment of either one's sense of equity and efficiency or in the extreme to the viability of the political process itself.

In this paper we present mechanisms for both direct and representative democracy that take into account the relative intensities of each voter's preference over issues.[1] In essence, we address the challenge posed by Dahl: "Is it possible to construct a system for arriving at decisions that is compatible with the idea of political equality and at the same time protects the rights of minorities?"[2]

The answer to this question can be found in neither of the two leading theories of American democracy, the Madisonian and Populist theories, as Dahl and others have shown.[3] The Populist theory, with its emphasis on the normative significance of one man-one vote majority rule, essentially ignores the problem, or implicitly assumes it away. Madisonian theory has as its greatest virtue the preservation of

* The authors are, respectively, Associate Professor of Economics, Cornell University; Associate Professor of Economics, Texas A&M University; and Assistant Secretary of the United States Treasury Department.

minority interests through the various "checks and balances" created in the constitution by the separation of the government into three branches, the separation of the legislature into two branches, and the decentralization of government into a federalist system. The strengthened position of the minority under Madisonian Democracy reduces the "tyranny of the majority" problem at the cost of creating a "tyranny of the minority," in which any lethargic minority can block the preferences of an intense majority. Although the American system is a blend of Populist and Madisonian democracy, few seem convinced that this blend has adequately resolved the dilemma between the two tyrannies of majority and minority control. Nor do we believe that the more modern theories of interest-group democracy and implicit mechanisms of bargaining between majorities and minorities provide a satisfactory answer.[4]

The solution to the intensity problem presented here combines elements of all of these theories. It is populist in that it requires that each voter have an *equal stake* (to be defined below) in the set of outcomes to be decided by any polity of which he is a member, and that he have an equal number of votes over the set of issues of the polity. It is Madisonian in requiring that the tasks of government be broken into separate branches, with particular emphasis placed on the judicial branch's control over the legislative through the delineation of political boundaries and issue sets. It emphasizes as well a federalist arrangement of government authority.

Our theory incorporates elements of the modern public-choice theories in that it starts from a set of assumed voter preferences over issues, and allows voters to satisfy these preferences by voting. In this sense we are presenting a generalization of the intensity problem which emphasizes a solution to the problem of voting for public goods that is analogous (subject to the constraint of majority rule on non-constitutional decisions) to the manner in which the market solves intensity problems for private goods. The model can also be adapted to allow for logrolling and bargaining.

This, of course, is not the only criterion for judging the desirability of government institutions. While in passing we do derive some of the effects which a more responsive voting mechanism might have on other attributes of desirable government institutions, we are not attempting to present a blueprint for the most desirable form of democratic institutions based on a careful weighing of all relevant criteria. We are attacking a much more limited question: how to design public-choice mechanisms to "solve" the intensity problem and accurately reflect in voting outcomes the underlying preferences of the electorate. This is an intriguing intellectual question in its own right and is not without practical implications. But while we feel that our "solution" to the intensity problem has important implications for the design of "good" democratic institutions, we wish to make very clear that we are not proposing a solution for all of the problems of democratic government.

In Section I we propose a direct democracy solution to the intensity problem that emphasizes giving voters a stock of votes to allocate over issues decided by a given polity. This process traces out relative utilities among issues for a voter and is called point voting.[5] Also, in Section I we discuss the requirement for the optimality of point voting in resolving the intensity problem, the equal-stake requirement.

In Section II we extend the advantages of point voting and the equal-stake requirement in representing the underlying structure of preferences to a form of representative government. We propose a system of at-large proportional representation for polities defined on the equal stake condition either with a legislator's vote stock proportioned to the number of votes he received in an election or with random selection of legislators each of whom receives one vote per issue.

In Section III we consider the kinds of constitutional decisions that are required in our model and some mechanisms for making them.

Sections IV and V contrast our model with the present system, discussing primarily the advantages of at-large versus geographic representation in Section IV and the possible effects of our model of proportional representation on party structure and stability of political parties in Section V.

Section VI presents a summary of the results of the paper.

I. RESOLVING THE INTENSITY PROBLEM IN DIRECT DEMOCRACY

In his review of the intensity problem Robert Dahl concludes by blankly stating that no solution exists.[6] In another well-known paper on the intensity problem Kendall and Carey stress that in a Madisonian form of democracy the intensity problem can be contained by deliberations between good-natured majorities and intense minorities, but that populistic democracy simply cannot solve the problem.[7] However, they also discuss problems caused in the Madisonian model by minorities taking advantage of majorities in the deliberative body by bluffing about the intensity of their feeling on issues, and their analysis of this problem stresses mechanisms to raise the cost of bluffing to minorities and the partial nature of resolutions of the problem along these lines. In this analysis they mention clearly the concepts of point voting and vote trading (p. 19), but never with respect to resolving the intensity problem. Indeed, they fail to grasp that in either Madisonian *or* Populistic models of democratic decision-making, point voting can resolve the intensity problem fully in an ideal sense and to an approximation in an operational sense. In the remainder of this section we apply point voting to resolve the intensity problem in direct democracy, and in Section II the solution is extended to a form of representative democracy.

As an example of the type of intensity problem that we

consider, take one of the simplest of all democratic processes: a local referendum to increase the property tax by a stated amount and use the funds to build a new school. This situation can easily lend itself to an intensity problem. For example, a majority of the voters may not have children and may be slightly opposed to the measure because of the (let us say) small tax increase that accompanies it. The parents of school-age children may be intensely for the school-tax package, however, because of the poor condition of the existing school. Thus, the parents would lose to a relatively indifferent majority in the defeat of the school issue. Conversely, one could envisage a situation in which the parents are in the majority, the proposed tax increase is substantial, the present school is in good condition, and the nonparents are "tyrannized" by the passage of the tax-school referendum. In either case the lesson is clear—for one man-one vote majority rule on separate issues to have normative authority, each voter must have an equal expected utility gain or loss from the outcome of any given issue. If this condition is not met, then voting, where each voter has one vote per issue, will not accurately reflect underlying voter preferences.

Kendall and Carey tend to characterize this type of electoral situation as a conflict between majority rule and political equality, emphasizing that its resolution may involve getting rid of majority rule *or* destroying political equality.[8] The solution to the intensity problem advanced here maintains majority rule for direct or legislative decision-making on non-constitutional issues, but broadens the definition of political equality under which majority rule prevails. As will be discussed with respect to the equal-stake requirement, the all-or-none trade-off between majority rule and political equality does not exist when political equality is defined over the whole set of issues to be decided by a polity rather than in terms of one vote per issue.

To clarify the example further, consider the distribution

of potential welfare or utility gains for a single voter over a set of n issues in Figure 1. The height of the curve is an index of the potential gain to the voter from a favorable outcome on that issue, where a favorable outcome may represent either the passage of a desired bill or defeat of an undesired bill. In order for there *not* to be a potential tyranny of the majority problem under majority rule, each voter must have the identical utility distribution as in Figure 1 (i.e., it is not enough for the integral to be the same; the utility distribution of voters must be identically distributed), with the only differences arising in whether they favor passage or defeat of an issue. For example, all voters must experience a y gain in utility from the outcome on issue x, although some voters receive the gain only if it passes and others only if it loses.

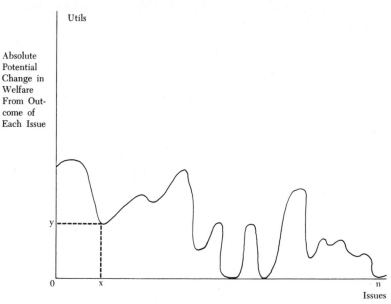

Utils

Absolute Potential Change in Welfare From Outcome of Each Issue

y

0 x n

Issues

FIGURE 1

Suppose, however, that all issues to be decided by a polity are formulated so that they can be decided by a yes or no vote. Each issue involving an expenditure is presented with a self-financing tax so that all voters know precisely the cost to them of the passage of a particular issue. Taking these costs into account, each voter determines his net benefits from the passage or defeat of every issue. These net benefits constitute the vertical distances given in Figure 1.

Now, instead of having one vote on each issue, suppose the voter is given a thousand votes and is asked to allocate these in proportion to his utility index over the n issues. Thus, if issue j provides seven times as much benefit as issue k, the voter allocates seven times as many votes to it. In voting he returns a form indicating how his thousand votes are to be assigned to each of the n issues and whether he casts them for or against each issue (he votes against all issues promising negative benefits). Ideally, each voter's allocation of votes will trace out a distribution exactly proportional to the utility distribution in Figure 1. The issues are decided by aggregating the vote distributions over all voters, and passing all issues that receive more yeses than noes.[9]

This type of "point-voting system" will give accurate information about the *relative* intensities of each voter's preferences over the n issues and thus removes the necessity of assuming that each voter has exactly the same relative utilities over the same n issues (i.e., that all voters have the same utility curve in Figure 1 except for signs). Operationally, the concept of point voting itself is not difficult to understand. This is particularly true for market economies where voters are faced with the same sort of allocation decisions in their market behavior. In the direct democracy variant the amount of sophistication required to allocate points over issues seems less demanding than the typical family's weekly budget decisions or the computations inherent in filling out a tax form.

Further, the use of point voting to resolve the intensity problem does not rely on implicit and indirect bargaining mechanisms between majorities and intense minorities to approximate, however inaccurately, the revelation of relative utilities in a political process. Point voting reveals relative intensities directly and in a theoretical sense both *solves* and *measures* the intensity problem straightforwardly.[10] In terms of the objective of reflecting the underlying array of voter preferences in public-choice outcomes, point voting-direct democracy reveals individuals' marginal rates of substitution among issues analogously to the manner in which marginal rates of substitution among private goods are revealed in markets as consumers allocate their budgets. In effect, point voting is the first step here in setting up a public-choice process that operates similarly to markets.

There is, however, an important condition which must be met for point voting to be completely optimal in an ideal sense. The social welfare W will be maximized by aggregating the votes cast by each citizen over the n issues *if and only if every voter has an equal total expected utility gain* from the outcome of the voting process over the *set* of n issues. This too is a strong condition. It is clearly unrealistic if the set of n issues consists of *all* the collective choices affecting a voter. An urban resident's welfare is more heavily dependent upon the outcomes of all political choices he can influence than is the farmer's. Many public services have a localized geographic effect, e.g., police and fire protection, education (particularly at the lower levels), recreation facilities, and health services. It is less unrealistic to assume, therefore, that the total set of issues affecting an individual can be broken down into subsets on a geographic basis, so that within each geographically determined polity all voters have an equal potential utility gain from the outcome of the decisions of that polity. That is, boundaries should be drawn for each neighborhood, city, regional, and national government such that all voters in any political jurisdiction have an equal expected utility gain over the subset of issues decided by that polity. Voters in each polity would be given an equal number of votes to be allocated among the issues decided by that polity.

One way of approaching the problem of drawing boundaries and allocating issues is to assume that these decisions are made at an earlier, constitutional stage in the democratic process. If one makes the further assumption that citizens at the constitutional stage are ignorant of their future tastes and positions, then the allocation of issues and boundaries so that voters have equal expected stakes becomes a necessary condition for maximizing social welfare at the constitutional stage. Under uniform ignorance about future preferences and positions *unanimous agreement* could be reached at the constitutional stage, and the equal-stake criterion, voting rules, redistributive measures, certain allocative measures such as contained in the Bill of Rights, etc., embodied in the Constitution could be regarded as the main elements of the social contract. With the equal-ignorance condition satisfied our approach to constitutional decision-making may be consistent with the Paretian criterion, since we could advance our proposed form of democratic decision-making as presumed Pareto-optimal at a constitutional convention and see if unanimous consensus could be found to support our model.[11]

Thus, the designation of political boundaries for each level of government and the allocation of issues among the various governments become key conditions in the creation of a voting system that accurately reflects relative intensities of preference among all groups in the polity. While we recognize that these conditions as a practical matter cannot be exactly met, we think that operational equivalents of these conditions (see n. 20), combined with the other mechanisms of the model, would be an improvement over other possible voting systems.

Previous theories that have failed to recognize these conditions have often encountered serious conceptual difficulties. The well-known Arrow Impossibility, where cycling can take place under majority rule, can be attributed to the fact that *all* citizens are allowed to participate in the making of *all* decisions, regardless of their interests in the outcomes of the process. Indeed, since point voting and vote trading are devices for combining *cardinal* utilities, intransitivities and cycling cannot occur as in the Arrow Impossibility, where with *ordinal* rankings there is no single alternative uniformly considered as the best, the worst, etc. Thus, cycling cannot occur because intransitivities are eliminated by introducing cardinality and because all issues are more or less decided at the same time. In effect, by basing the optimality of the point-voting system on the characteristic of voters deciding all issues simultaneously at either the parliamentary or constitutional stage of the model, the Arrow Impossibility is bypassed by violating his postulate of the independence of irrelevant alternatives.[12]

This part of the theory is quite consistent with traditional American political thought. The defense of minority rights through guarantees of local political authority was one of the major issues in the drafting of the Constitution.[13] The condition that every voter have an equal stake in the outcomes over the set of issues affecting him also seems fully consistent with America's populist democratic traditions. Again, however, its importance has not been fully recognized in the literature and its violation in the large is probably a major cause of frustration with the democratic process. When issues are decided with vote trading or logrolling, the outcomes on *all* issues are interdependent and sensitive to the selection of issues. The addition of issues to the choice set (e.g., that would hurt some groups and leave the others unaffected) can lower the realized utility gains of the former groups even if the added issues are eventually defeated because the potentially injured voters must trade away votes on the potentially harmful issues to insure their defeat, and thereby lower their power to affect other decisions that might benefit them. The selection of issues is also important under

point voting. The addition of an issue to the set alters the
vote-point allocations and has a potential impact on all
outcomes. Care must be taken when selecting the issues to
be voted upon to ensure that all voters stand to experience
roughly equal utility gains from the outcomes of the decision process.[14]

A number of papers have explored the possibilities of
getting voters to reveal the relative intensities of their preferences by trading votes.[15] Mueller, Philpotts and Vanek have
shown in a polar version of this model in which voters
literally do trade votes (or fractions thereof) in vote markets, that the outcomes from vote trading closely approximate
those one would obtain under point voting.[16] Although it
is a long leap from this kind of vote trading to the implicit
trading that takes place via logrolling in actual assemblies,
at least one observer has been willing to argue that logrolling
tends to approximate the results one would get with actual
trading.[17] Thus, the results we seek might tend to be approxi-
mated via some form of vote trading without having to
resort to point voting *if the equal-stake criterion were satisfied and proportional representation were adopted* (we discuss the latter condition in the next section).

Most criticisms of the actual results of logrolling can be
traced directly to the violation of the equal-stake criterion.
The ill effects of pork-barrel legislation come about because
those with very small stakes in the total set of issues to be
decided can trade away votes on all but the relatively few
issues they consider important and thus ensure their victory
to the likely detriment of the community at large. The tendency of these asymmetries to exist, and for local issues to
gravitate to higher levels of government, is enhanced by
the geographic selection of representatives. We will consider
the effects of geographic representation on the propensity
of legislators to play negative-sum games in more detail
in Section IV.

II. EXTENDING THE SOLUTION TO
REPRESENTATIVE DEMOCRACY

If point voting were employed at each level of government, and legislative decisions at each level were made via direct democracy, then the utility distributions of each voter as depicted in Figure 1 would be employed directly in the legislative process. All of the available information about the relative intensities of voter preferences on issues would be utilized in legislative decision making by a point voting-direct democracy.

Direct democracy is often impractical, however.[18] Historically, town meetings were reasonably efficient in a small numbers setting. As society grew and the number of voters became large, direct assembly and debate became difficult, and the deliberative step in the legislative process was not viable in a direct form of democracy. Today, as issues become more complex, the amount of information needed to vote intelligently increases and it becomes inefficient to have each voter gather all the necessary information himself. Thus, representative government is superior to direct democracy, chiefly because of the greater informational efficiency inherent in it. The standard institutions of representative bodies such as committees, staffs, hearings, and the like are all embodiments of this point.

We seek a method for choosing representatives that will preserve the advantages of point voting in revealing the relative intensities of individual preferences and still incorporates the informational efficiency of representative government. This can be accomplished if each voter selects a legislator who will *represent* his general preferences on the issues, given the greater information the latter will typically have. Each voter must thus choose a representative who promises to take positions on the issues in rough correspondence to the voter's preference map. If the voters in a polity can be broken down into a number of sub-groups each of which is composed of voters of homogeneous tastes (identical preference maps), then each voter can have his tastes accurately represented in the legislature if a representative is chosen from his sub-group. Suppose, for example, that the m voters in a city can be divided into s subsets of $v_1, v_2, \ldots v_s$ voters, respectively, where the members of any subset have identical preferences. Then, ideally, a perfectly representative body could be established by selecting s representatives, one each from the s subsets of voters. If point voting were employed in the legislature, each representative could accurately depict the relative intensities of his constituents on the issues. In order to make the aggregation of points an accurate reflection of the aggregate gains and losses from deciding each issue, the total numbers of vote-points representatives received would have to be proportioned to the number of votes they represented. Thus, the representatives could start with numbers of points proportional to $v_1, v_2, \ldots v_s$.

If voter preferences are such that voters in any polity can be grouped into a number of subsets of voters with homogeneous tastes that is sufficiently small to allow the creation of an assembly with a single representative from each subset, then the informational efficiency of point voting can be extended to a representative form of government. The representatives to the legislative branches at each level of government would have to be selected from a list of at-large candidates presented to all the voters in the several polities. The x seats in each legislature would be filled by the x candidates receiving the most votes, and each candidate would receive a number of vote-points proportioned to the number of seats in the assembly. Voting in the legislature would take place following the same point-voting scheme described in Section I. The points cast by a representative would give the relative intensities of his constituents weighted by their number.[19]

Additional flexibility can be added to the selection of

representatives to the various levels of government by using a form of point voting to select representatives. That is, instead of giving each voter one vote to cast for a representative at each level of government, voters could be given *m* votes to allocate to the representatives over all levels of government. In this way, voters could express their relative intensities of preference *within* each level of government by voting for those candidates who had platforms most closely resembling their own, and *across* levels of government by allocating their points for selecting representatives in proportion to their relative intensities of preference on the different levels. The latter allocation would give more political power to those representatives elected at the levels of government about which the voter felt more strongly. A modified form of the equal-stake criterion would now be required in which each voter in a *local* polity received the same number of points to be allocated to representatives to *all* polities of which he was a member. Since urban dwellers will typically receive greater benefits from the political process than rural dwellers (they are affected by more social interdependence and market failures), urban dwellers will have to receive more total points, although within any urban area (or within a neighborhood of an urban area if that is the lowest political unit) all voters would receive the same number of votes.[20] This modification to the electoral process would require more information on the part of the construction of the initial boundaries, since not only would boundaries giving equal stakes be required, but also decisions as to the *relative* intensities of total utility gains among voters in different areas would have to be made. On the other hand, it is less restrictive in its constraints on voter preferences, since it only requires that voters in the same local community receive an equal utility gain over the set of *all* issues affecting them. The optimality of election of representatives by one man-one vote assumes equal utility gains for voters in the same local area over *each* set of issues affecting him.

A system for proportionately *electing* legislators to each level of government would make greater demand on the abilities of voters to gather and evaluate information about candidates. If, for example, the national assembly had 100 seats, the voter might have to evaluate 150 candidates (including the primary election) in deciding which one would best represent his views. Similar evaluations would have to be made when he selected his representatives to the state (regional), metropolitan, and neighborhood legislatures. If information were supplied to voters in the same way as it is today, his task in evaluating candidates might be impossible.

Fortunately, under proportional representation candidates will have incentives to provide more accurate information to voters. Under a two-party system where only one candidate emerges as a winner, candidates have an incentive to take positions close to the median voter's position and to cloud their stands on controversial (polar) seats. Under proportional representation, candidates compete for a much larger number of seats and need to secure a much smaller number of votes to be elected. Their incentives are, therefore, to differentiate their positions from those of other candidates and convince voters that their platforms most closely correspond to the voter's own preferences.

A simple way to supply voters with information about candidates would be to publish a manual that listed each incumbent candidate and his allocations of vote points in the preceding congresses. Challengers could list the way they would allocate their vote points once in office as opposed to the incumbent's proposed allocation. More radical innovations in the use of the media to supply voters with information about candidates could also be considered.

There would remain, however, after these improvements in information flow, a trade-off between the number of candidates and decision-making costs faced by the representative individual voter, as Figure 2 illustrates.

The decision-costs function in this case would increase

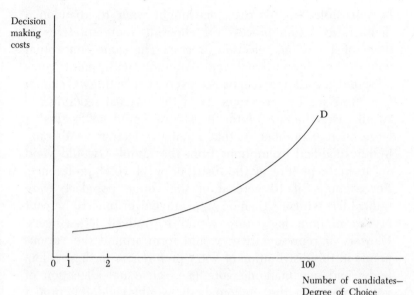

FIGURE 2

at an increasing rate as more candidates imposed greater
complexity on the choice facing the voter. Thus, the trade-
off between having a large legislature to reflect voters' tastes
more accurately and decision-making costs for voters would
be present in any democratic system where voter participation is required. Selecting a point on this trade-off curve
would determine a voter's trade-off between the amount
of choice he desires in selecting a representative and the
cost of making this choice. One suspects that in a complex
society with a highly educated and wealthy population the
optimal trade-off point is somewhere to the right of the
two-party point, and it probably shifts to the right over
time as the society develops.

It is possible, nevertheless, that the number of seats needed
to reflect adequately the spectrum of individual preferences
is so large, that a proportionally elected assembly fully representative of the full range of individual preferences would

be infeasible. In this case, one might want to abandon a democratic voting process for choosing representatives in favor of a random selection process. The same conceptual outcome as proportional representation with point votes allocated accordingly can be achieved by selecting *at random* legislators for the governments in the rational federalism.[21] In all cases the size of the legislature could be fixed at a large enough number so that random selection (with only highly qualified exemptions from the sample) would yield an accurate picture of the distribution of voter preference. For example, if 10 percent of the voting populace were radical left-wingers, then on an average over time 10 percent of the random legislature would be radical left-wingers. Clusters of representatives would form around the various points in the distribution of voter preferences in the random body, and one man-one vote (i.e., an equal allocation of vote points) in the random body would yield the proper proportional weights to the various intensities of voter preference. The selected representatives could then still allocate their stock of one vote per issue in any way they chose, i.e., point voting. In such fashion the random selection system would yield the *same conceptual* result as proportional representation with vote points allocated accordingly.

Representation by random selection would return political power to individual voters and give better articulation of voter preferences in the legislative process without sacrificing the efficiencies of representation. If viewed as a replacement for the current forms of national representation, the random selection system removes direct sanctioning power through the ballot from the voter and replaces this control mechanism with a more subtle method of articulating voter preferences on national issues. We would argue that although the final outcome is not clear cut, such a change in representative procedure could be understood by voters as the formal embodiment of democratic equality in an *ex ante* rather than *ex post* sense.[22] Finally, and importantly, it should be stressed that random selection of representatives avoids all of the traditional problems in voting theory of intransitivities in voting outcomes in establishing a system of proportional representation.[23] The application of voting theory is confined in this case to the operation of the random legislature, once selected, and this feature of random representation is an important justification for establishing and operating proportional representation in this way.

In summary, both a *proportionally elected* assembly that employed point voting and a *randomly selected* assembly would provide an accurate depiction of the preferences of the population if they were large enough relative to the spectrum of preferences of the voters. In the former assembly each subset of preferences would be represented by a single representative who would have a total number of vote points to allocate over issues in proportion to the number of voters he represented. Under the random selection process each representative would have the same number of vote points, and the different numbers of voters in each preference subset would be revealed through the random selection process. The choice between these two systems must rest basically on (1) the advantages of having all voters *participate* in democracy by *electing* a representative versus having an *equal chance* to be selected as a representative, and (2) the range of preferences of voters and the costs of making decisions among candidates. It should be noted, however, that both proposals have inherent in them an increase in the amount of information about issues that the average citizen possesses. Under the proportional election system *all* voters would be expected to incur greater decision costs in selecting representatives. Under the random selection process those citizens chosen to be representatives would have to acquire information about issues at least during their term of office.

Although there is no need for a bicameral legislature if conditions are appropriate for either of the above two representative schemes, one might want to adopt a bicameral system to capture the best features of both, especially if these conditions are not met. Random selection could be used to select a large proportionally representative body, and proportional voting to elect a much smaller body. The smaller body would be responsible for initiating, debating, and amending legislation, and the large body would serve as a fully representative cross-section of the population with veto power over the elected assembly. The smaller assembly could also serve as the home ground for political entrepreneurs.

Finally, we should stress that on the assumption of homogeneous tastes among blocs of voters and the satisfaction of the equal-stake requirement for the various polities implied in our model, the solution of the intensity problem is carried over to a representative setting. The underlying array of preferences is reflected in voting outcomes in a proportionally representative legislature, and issues are decided at the correct level of government by optimal jurisdictions based on the satisfaction of the equal-stake requirement. The latter conditions of agenda setting and drawing the boundaries of governments raise the important problems of constitutional decision-making which we consider in the next section.

III.   CONSTITUTIONAL DECISIONS

The selection of issues and delineation of boundaries for each level of government is such an important component of our theory that some discussion of the method by which these decisions would be made is necessary.

One must quickly reject any existing legislative bodies for this task, at least under current voting rules. Representatives are now selected geographically, and one would expect that any decisions made by an existing legislature would tend to preserve present asymmetries in political power among different areas and the tendency to kick local issues up to the national level. The U.S. Constitution's strong emphasis on preserving the power of certain geographic areas can be traced directly to the selection of delegates to the Constitutional Convention on a geographic basis. More recently, the Bretton Woods agreement on the international monetary system set up after World War II is a good example of such short-sighted behavior by rule makers, with the positions of major powers being strongly influenced by their expectations as to whether they would have balance of payments surpluses or deficits over the early post-war years.[24] Indeed, since the whole idea of the equal-stakes assumption is to straighten out geographic biases currently prevailing, it is hard to see how we could get any part of the existing political system to make correct constitutional choices unless the choices were not to take effect until a time so distant, say three generations hence, that they would be irrelevant to the current reform of democratic decision-making. And it would be extremely hard, if not impossible, for any existing political body to resist overcentralizing geographic issues.

One way out of this dilemma would be to hold a constitutional convention with delegates selected by proportional representation with the point-voting method or via random selection. These procedures would lessen the geographic incentives toward overcentralization and would at least yield a constitutional reform based on the full range of voter preferences. For example, selecting the delegates at random and allowing the decisions to take effect only after an elapsed period of time might obviate many of the problems here. In a sense, we are trying to solve the intensity problem in a constitutional setting and also to obtain a constitutional state of mind of uniform ignorance about everyone's future position in the society (see n. 8).

The partisanship inherent in the geographic selection of representatives is reinforced by the possibility of representatives running for re-election. This kind of partisanship may be desirable with regard to the day-to-day decisions of a legislature, since it provides the citizen a means of ensuring that his views are in fact being represented in the democratic process. It is not suitable, however, for obtaining the kind of disinterestedness called for in establishing the equal-stake requirement. The typical way in which the Constitution seeks to ensure impartiality in decision-making by an officer is to preclude his concern with selection or reappointment. Thus, judges on the highest courts are appointed for life, governors on the Federal Reserve Board and Commissioners in the regulatory agencies are appointed for fixed, nonrenewable terms, and jurors are selected randomly and for fixed time periods. In a similar manner, impartiality could be obtained in settling jurisdictional issues in a federal system and constructing a new form of representative body. A constitutional convention could be called, and either of the two methods of selecting representatives described above could be used; i.e., representatives could be randomly drawn or voted on from an at-large list of candidates. What is essential is that they do not have to run for re-election on the basis of the *justice* they exhibit in drawing the federation's local and regional boundaries and allocating issues.

Two primary tasks of the convention would be to draw political boundaries to approximate the equal-stake criterion and to allocate issues to the appropriate level of federalism. In effect, the setting of the equal-stake requirement and the allocating of issues to the appropriate level set the income distribution requirements of the model, and the model at this point would be analogous to setting an equitable income distribution and letting the market work, though again with majority rule arbitrating legislative decisions.

In addition, an important function of the convention would be to decide whether an issue is constitutional in an *ex ante* sense. This is the manner in which issues (intense minority-intense majority) that can potentially break down the system and traditional items in the Bill of Rights could be handled, if they are foreseen at the time of the convention. In the latter case, all-or-none rules could be set up at the convention outlawing or sanctioning certain rights. If such issues are not foreseen, then the convention would be faced with the task of setting up constitutional procedures to take effect in the future to resolve such issues.

This task of setting up future constitutional machinery should be broadly construed. For example, Braybrooke has an interesting test to allow individuals to be in a winning *or* losing coalition only 90 percent of the time that would qualify in our terms as a constitutional device. In effect this would be a system of progressive taxation of political income that could be imposed by a constitutional convention to lessen the problems of persistent majorities over future political periods, i.e., the long-run form of the intensity problem.[25]

Two possibilities exist for arbitrating future jurisdictional disputes. The constitutional convention could be reconvened periodically to take up the redrawing of boundaries and allocation of issues in light of changing population densities and environmental factors. In this way the convention would function as a sort of jury for deciding federalism issues. Alternatively, the equal-stake criterion could be broadly written into Federal and State constitutions, and the courts could be relied upon to draw the boundaries in an equitable manner. Clearly, the recurring constitutional convention approach is time-consuming and costly and perhaps not flexible enough to apply in the modern world. The judicial approach meets these objections, but poses problems of how one selects the judges in a way that is totally free of interest-group bias. In essence, efficiency considerations probably imply movement toward more judicial democracy so long as the judges are selected in a way to reflect accurately the distribution of voter preference.[26] An effective way to combine the judicial approach to redrawing boundaries and allocating issues with our electoral proposals would be to maintain a small random jury of judges to make such decisions over time.

Such a procedure could be set up to function independently of other governmental institutions in the spirit of Madisonian checks and balances. Thus, the important constitutional tasks of drawing political boundaries and setting legislative agendas would fall to an independent judicial body. This constitutional body, if selected in such a way as to offset any short-run geographic bias in decision-making, would serve to check tendencies for the legislative branch to over-centralize issues (discussed in the next section).

IV. PROBLEMS OF GEOGRAPHIC REPRESENTATION

Our model has four central characteristics: (1) point voting to reveal relative intensities of preference over a set of issues; (2) a federation of governments such that every citizen in a given polity has an equal expected welfare gain from the set of outcomes in that polity; (3) an active judiciary or constitution-drafting process for redrawing political boundaries and screening issue sets to ensure that the equal-stakes criterion is satisfied in each polity; and (4) at-large proportional representation through either proportionally elected or randomly selected legislative bodies.

A primary difference in the model presented here and the present American political system is that of at-large versus geographic representation. We will thus contrast in this section some of the problems caused by geographic representation under the present system with the at-large representation system implied in the foregoing model.

Under geographic representation the main characteristic a representative's constituents have in common is that they reside in the same area. Any bill he can get through the legislature that benefits all of the members of his district should win him votes. In effect, a geographic-based system confronts the legislator with high pay-offs from representing local interests in the national legislature by trying to logroll off, for example, the general tax system, and with virtually zero pay-offs to campaign on a platform, for example, of national efficiency. This asymmetry in pay-off to the geographic-based legislator is partly attributable to the greater information voters have about localized and specific public-sector benefits than about more remote general benefits.[27] Coupled with a seniority system in the legislature, which gives monopoly power on important committees (e.g., in terms of which issues are put on committee agendas) to those districts that send back the same representative over a long period of time, the problem of representing local interests in the national legislature is compounded because legislative survival and the attainment of monopoly power within the legislature become functions of representing local interests.

One of the most important concerns individuals in a community have in common is their interest in the vitality of the community's economic base. In many instances a majority of the members of a polity may directly or indirectly receive their income from a single firm or industry. Company towns; geographically concentrated industries like steel, autos, textiles, lumber, defense; and regionally concentrated agricultural industries are all examples of this. When economic activity is thus concentrated, it is possible for representatives to win political support by serving as spokesmen for the economic interests in their home districts. Tariffs, industry and company-oriented tax concessions and subsidies, local public-works projects, and defense contracts are all examples of issues that often are decided, in part, on the basis of their economic impact on certain regions.

Such attempts to redistribute income toward certain regions through the legislative process frequently result in negative-sum games. Examples of this kind of negative-sum game legislation in the form of tariffs, Department of the Interior pork-barrel public works legislation, Christmas-tree tax "reform" bills, and so forth, are replete in legislative history.[28]

What is bad about this form of logrolling, at say the

national level, is not that it acts as a means for revealing relative intensities of preferences on national issues—indeed, this is essential if one is to avoid the imposition of the will of passive majorities over intense minorities—but that in its most blatant forms it is used to reveal relative intensities of preference on essentially local issues that never should come before the national legislature. When restricted to positive-sum games, logrolling can become a beneficial means for revealing voter preferences on issues. This confusion as to whether logrolling applies to positive or negative-sum games can help to explain the disagreements among many observers over the benefits from logrolling.[29]

Our model would reduce the likelihood that legislatures would engage in negative-sum games in two ways. First, at-large representation eliminates the direct link between a representative and local interests. Although he can still adopt platforms based on local issues, the legislative candidate would have an incentive to broaden his appeal to a larger constituency in order to increase the number of votes he receives. Candidates who stressed economy in government, free trade, consumer protection and similar positive-sum game issues would be able to increase their political strength under proportional representation by appealing directly to a national constituency (for example, by proposing the potential tax reductions inherent in such platforms).

The control over the issue-selection process by the judicial branch provides the second check on the legislative branch's engaging in negative-sum games. Bills that favored special economic or geographic interests would not be allowed on the agenda because of the likelihood that they violate the equal-stake criterion. They would be channeled, along with intense majority-intense minority issues, into the constitutional amendment process. Although this may sound novel, it is quite consistent with the spirit of the Constitution. The right to engage in commerce is guaranteed by the Constitution, but it is emasculated by tariffs, quotas, state and privately enforced monopolies, etc. Given a choice between a free trade-free competition bill and a Christmas tree tariff-monopoly-monopsony bill, a constitutional convention bound by an unanimity rule should select the former. Similarly, it was deemed necessary to pass a constitutional amendment to enable the government to tax personal income. Yet, the defining of income and selection of tax rates was left up to legislative logrolling, thereby eliminating the equity implicit in the constitutional sanction for the tax. The way, the only conceivable way, to achieve horizontal and vertical equity in the definition of income and tax rates, is to decide these issues by some form of judicial process. A constitutional convention charged with the responsibility of establishing an equitable income tax might come up with such a tax, if its members could adopt a sufficient degree of detachment so that they weighted the tax's likely impact on all citizens, and if they did not have to run for re-election by appealing for the votes of a certain subset of the citizens. Once established, all changes in tariff, monopoly, and income tax policy would be made by the same constitutional process under unanimous consent, thereby ensuring the positive-sum nature of any changes.[30]

When this process for selecting issues is contrasted with the present system in which small committees of the legislature determine the issue set, the composition of the committees is relatively stable over time, the legislators are selected geographically and often favor special local and economic interests, and the seniority system allows certain regions and localities to have more power within the committees than others, one gets a far different picture of the likelihood of negative-sum game playing in the legislature.

V.   STABILITY AND PARTIES

Another primary difference between the model and the present American political system is that the performance of the latter is strongly determined by the outcomes achieved under a two-party system of government, while the model presented here emphasizes a multi-party system. The issue of stability has been raised with respect to multi-party systems in at least two senses. First, in the literature on the economic theory of democracy the stability of party positions along an ideological spectrum has been questioned (see n. 31). Second, on pragmatic and empirical grounds the "stability of the government" under a multi-party system is often questioned. We discuss both these issues in this section, although primary attention is given to the first.

It is well known that under a two-party system candidates tend to take median positions. Assume, for example, preferences on issues can be depicted as lying along a spectrum running from radical left to reactionary right as in Figure 3. If one party's candidate adopts the median position, M, he guarantees himself at least a tie in the election. If the second party's candidate adopts any other position, e.g., R, he will get less than 50 percent of the votes if each citizen votes for the candidate closest to him. Thus, the best strategy for the second party candidate is to adopt the same position as the other candidate, M, and hope that by random error on the part of voters, he emerges a winner.

Note what happens if a third-party candidate enters the race, however. If he adopts R, while the other two are at M, he gets all votes to the right of R and half of those between M and R, and beats both of the other candidates. This should induce one of the other two candidates to move from M to, say, L, isolating the candidate at M with a small fraction of the vote. The candidate at M will then have an incentive to move outside of the L-R segment, thereby trapping one of the other candidates and so on. Starting from a position in which all candidates are at the center, at least one candidate in a multi-party (more than two) system will have an incentive to move away from the center.

In the extreme, one can envisage this spreading out to continue until the total range is covered and each candidate

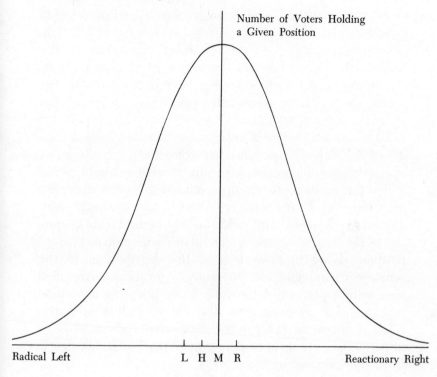

Number of Voters Holding
a Given Position

Radical Left   L   H   M   R   Reactionary Right

FIGURE 3

receives an identical fraction of the vote. In a 100-man legislature, each candidate would locate at the center of a percentile, and receive 1 percent of the vote. Starting from
this distribution of positions, however, candidates will have
an incentive to move back toward the center. With the
peak in the center, a candidate can increase his percentage
of the vote by moving slightly toward the center. This can
be seen in Figure 3 by noting that with candidates at L, M,
and R, the two outside candidates can increase their votes
by moving toward M.

Thus, in general, the positioning of the candidates along
an ideological spectrum in a multi-party system is unstable.[31]
Depending upon the starting point, there may be incentives

to move toward the center or away from it, and movements in both directions could be occurring at the same time. (The situation is analogous to the instability that occurs in the Edgeworth duopoly model. Starting from the joint profit-maximizing price each duopolist has an incentive to cut prices; starting from competitive price, each duopolist has an incentive to raise prices.)

There are a number of reasons for believing that a considerable (although perhaps not complete) spreading out of candidates along the left-right spectrum would occur under the multi-party (multi-candidate) system discussed here, however. In the primary in which, say, 150 to 200 candidates are entered, and only the 100 highest vote getters are in the final slate, many candidates will probably adopt positions along the two tails of the distribution. In the primary a candidate can guarantee a position in the final slate with 1 percent of the vote. Thus, adopting a position relatively far removed from the other candidates, unless it is way out on the tail, can get one elected. New candidates, in particular, will want to differentiate their positions clearly from the incumbents.

Let us assume that the candidates do apportion themselves along the political spectrum, so that following the primary each of the 100 winning candidates is in the middle of a percentile of voters. Each now faces the strategy choices of moving toward the center or staying put (see Table 1). If he stays and all other candidates stay, he is assured of 1 percent of the vote. If he moves in the direction of the median immediately beside the adjacent candidate, and all other candidates stay, he increases his share of the vote to somewhere between one and one-and-a-half percent. If all other candidates adopt a similar strategy, and the process is followed to completion, all arrive at M with expected shares of the vote all equal to 1 percent with voters randomly choosing among the candidates.

The case in which all other candidates move and one

TABLE 1

Candidate L	All other candidates stay	All other candidates move beside the next candidate toward the center
Stays	$S = 1\%$	$S = \int_{-\infty}^{H} f(X)\, dX$
Moves next to the candidate to his immediate right	$1\% < S < 1.5\%$	$E(S) = 1\%$

$S =$ candidate L's share of the vote
$f(X) =$ frequency distribution

stays in place is a little more complicated. Suppose L is the candidate who stays in place. All candidates to his right move to M, and L gets the percentage of the vote represented by the area under the curve between L and H, a point halfway between L and M. All candidates to the left of him move to his immediate left. The expected percentage of votes for one of these candidates is now slightly greater than 1 percent. Any one of them can increase his percentage of the vote by jumping L and taking the furthest position to the left of M in the bunch at the center. If all other candidates on the left do this, L is left alone to the left of M and gets all votes to the left of H.

If we assume candidates prefer the certain 1 percent they achieve if all candidates stay to the risky 1 percent they can expect if they all plunge into the center, the stay strategy is preferred under the maximin criterion. Although the instability of the outcomes when all or almost all are moving places a high variance around the pay-offs in the second column, the rather high pay-off from staying in place in the polar example should dominate and make staying the preferred strategy under most decision rules. Only if a high probability is placed on other candidates staying will moving toward the center produce a slight expected gain.

The attractiveness of moving is still further reduced once possible voter reactions are introduced. A risk-averting voter may prefer a candidate who steadily maintains a position somewhat near his own, to one who is currently at the voter's position, but is constantly moving. To the extent that voters favor candidates who adopt (or appear to adopt) attitudes out of conviction rather than as strategies for winning votes, shifting positions is further discouraged.[32] Finally, the already difficult task of acquainting voters with one's platform, when there is a long list of candidates, will be made even more difficult if the candidate is constantly changing his position.

Thus, under the proposed form of proportional representation the candidates would tend to spread out along the full spectrum of preferences and remain in their positions under plausible conditions, in contrast to the two-party outcome. Each voter could select a candidate close to his own position; each voter would be assured that the candidate he voted for in the final election would be in the legislature to represent him. And with a randomly selected legislature, at least some of the chosen members would probably be close to any individual voter's position.

When only one winner is selected from each district, parties that are thinly spread across a country will not win seats in an election. Since it is hard for parties out of office to remain viable, the ins and outs characteristic of geographic representation reduce the number of parties over time to those with sufficient geographic concentration to win some seats in assemblies. On the other hand, any party with some national following, no matter how it is dispersed geographically, can elect some representatives to the national assembly under at-large proportional representation or random selection, and thereby maintain its visibility, credibility, and existence.[33]

Under a proportionally representative system the importance of political parties would probably decline. The two-party system would most certainly be replaced by a multi-party structure, and even within parties it would be the individual platforms of the candidates that would determine the number of votes they got. Party designations might aid voters in concentrating on those subsets of candidates that are most likely to approximate their views, but the same kind of information could be provided by subdividing the voter's manual by ideological position (liberal-conservative, hawk-dove, segregationist-integrationist).

One of the chief pragmatic virtues claimed for the two-party system is stability.[34] This stability stems from the tendency of two-party democracy to satisfy the middle voters by producing median outcomes and comes at the expense of frustrating the voters on both tails of the political spectrum. In times of profound ideological disagreement, when the middle ground gives way to an enlarging of the numbers of voters at the two extremes, the frustration produced by two-party democracy may produce political instability, however, and even the demise of the two-party system. The political history of the United States is replete with examples of third and fourth parties forming out of the frustration of a lack of voice under the two-party system.[35] At-large proportional representation or random selection would institutionalize the multi-party framework and provide all minority groups of moderate size a legitimate voice in the political process.

With respect to the second type of stability problem raised by a multi-party system ("stability of the government"), it should be noted that proportional representation need not result in the political instability that characterizes some multi-party parliamentary governments. The chief executive could still be elected for a fixed term of office, with impeachment a difficult and rare occurrence. Stability could thus be preserved in the executive branch.[36]

V. SUMMARY AND CONCLUSION

The preferences of minorities can be reflected under majority rule by giving each voter an equal number of vote points which he can allocate over all issues in proportion to his relative intensity of preference. The information needed to make decisions in a modern, urban society precludes the gathering of information on voter preferences by direct democracy. Still, the advantages of direct democracy-point voting in reflecting voter preferences can be preserved by selecting representatives to each legislature in proportion to the number of voters in each polity having similar preferences. As an added advantage, the selection of legislators on an at-large basis would reduce the link between concentrated economic power and political power that geographic representation aids in producing. Further, under plausible conditions about voter and party behavior, the multi-party system implied in our model would be stable.

The optimality of proportional representation with point voting rests heavily upon a requirement that political boundaries be drawn and issues allocated among polities so that each voter in a polity has an equal potential utility gain from that polity's decision. This equal-stake criterion is quite consistent with the populist spirit of American democracy, but again places several requirements on the way fiscal federalism decisions are resolved. Indeed, the impartiality required in the equal-stake condition could only be achieved by a judicial or quasi-judicial body, like the courts or a constitutional convention. Thus the political system which we discuss would place increased demands on the judicial process, as well as on the legislative process, and the citizens themselves. But, such shifts in power will obviously be necessary under any attempt to strengthen democracy by returning power to the people.

NOTES

1. Our proposal may not resolve the type of problem where, for example, an intense majority faces an intense minority on an issue (e.g., racism). This sort of issue is not strictly an intensity problem, but rather a problem perhaps best characterized as a "crisis of the state," where resort to a constitutional setting is generally regarded as necessary and one constitutional option is the division of the state. As noted, such issues should be resolved at the constitutional stage where, ideally, citizens take a longer run, more disinterested view of outcomes. The references cited in n. 3 recognize the need of recourse to constitutional procedures in such cases. We discuss constitutional decision-making in Section III and n. 14 below. In addition to the type of intensity problem described in the text, there is also the possibility that even in a well working democratic model such as the one presented in this paper, there can be long-run *persistent* majorities and minorities. Thus, even where relative intensities on issues can be taken into account (*ex ante*) in setting up a democratic system, there can still be permanent winners and losers over time (*ex post*). We discuss this type of intensity problem in more detail in Section III (n. 25) and in a separate paper entitled "On Equalizing the Distribution of Political Income," *Journal of Political Economy*, 82 (March/April, 1974): 414-22.

2. Robert A. Dahl, *A Preface to Democratic Theory* (Chicago: University of Chicago Press, 1956), p. 90.

3. *Ibid*. See also Wilmoore Kendall and George W. Carey, "The 'Intensity' Problem and Democratic Theory," *American Political Science Review*, 62 (March, 1968): 4-24; and V. Ostrom, *The Political Theory of a Compound Republic*, Center for the Study of Public Choice, 1971.

4. For a discussion of implicit mechanisms, see Kendall and Carey, *op. cit.*, 16–19, and some of the literature on logrolling cited in n. 15.

5. To our knowledge the point-voting scheme was first proposed by Musgrave in *The Theory of Public Finance* (New York: McGraw-Hill, 1959), pp. 130–31. Coleman discusses the concept of point voting, but cites no precedent discussion and never analyzes the concept. See his "Political Money," *American Political Service Review*, 64 (December, 1970): 1074–87. Kendall and Carey, *op. cit.*, p. 19, mention point voting, but never with respect to resolving the intensity problem. Also, Zeckhauser has discussed some problems in the use of lotteries as an alternative way to handle varying intensities of voters' preference. See R. Zeckhauser, "Majority Rule with Lotteries on Alternatives," *Quarterly Journal of Economics*, 83 (November, 1968): 696–703.

6. Dahl, *op. cit.*, p. 119.

7. Kendall and Carey, *op. cit.* For example, they state that "Put

otherwise: it remains true, as a matter of history, that the intensity problem has arisen as a special problem in the theory of populistic democracy; but it has not, on our showing here, arisen there properly, because populistic democracy has no hooks for grappling with it" (p. 11).

8. *Ibid.*, pp. 5–7.

9. See n. 5.

10. Dahl, *op. cit.*, Chapter 4, is especially concerned with the problem of measuring differing intensities of preference as an issue. The point-voting system does this directly in the sense of revealed preference.

11. For a further discussion linking the voting rules and boundaries of parliamentary democracy to the constitutional decision, see D. Mueller, "Fiscal Federalism in a Constitutional Democracy," *Public Policy*, XIX (Fall, 1971): 567-93; and "Constitutional Democracy and Social Welfare," *Quarterly Journal of Economics*, 87 (February, 1973): 60-80. In practice, of course, one would not get the ideal solution even if the appropriate measurements for boundaries could be made because such factors as transactions costs would have to be traded off against the gains from setting up exactly optimum governments. In operation, say in the U.S., most of the changes in governmental boundaries would probably be at the metropolitan and regional levels. See Tullock, "Federalism: Problems of Scale," *Public Choice*, 6 (Spring, 1969): 19-29, for an example of the discussion of transaction costs. Mueller points out that a certain amount of "good citizenship" by voters is required if point voting is to reveal individuals' marginal rates of substitution among issues. In a large number setting such behavior is plausible. In a small number setting, for example, a small representative legislature, all voting systems are subject to strategic voting, and it is an open question whether point voting is better or worse in this regard than, for example, are one man–one vote systems. We will return to this problem in the next section.

We also note that in the discussions of the intensity problem the prospect of non-voting also raises the general problem of the representativeness of collective decisions under majority rule, and there may be cases where a polity would wish to enforce participation via a poll tax or subsidy as a way to internalize any publicness involved with attaining the full expression of underlying voter preferences. Then, the intensity problem could be solved by point voting, and representation of underlying preferences would be "full." Also, the empirical form of the potential bias due to non-voting is that voting and political participation tend to vary positively with income. For discussions of the economic theory of voting and non-voting behavior, see R. D. Tollison and T. D. Willett, "Some Simple Economics of Voting and Not Voting," *Public Choice*, 16 (Fall, 1973): 59-71, and the references cited there.

12. For Arrow's discussion see his *Social Choice and Individual Values* (New York: John Wiley, 1951). Also see Mishan's criticism of Arrow with regard to allowing all voters a stake in all decisions in "A Survey of Welfare Economics: 1939–1959," *Economic Journal,* 70 (June, 1970): 197–265. For the full discussion of how point voting avoids the Arrow Impossibility, see Mueller, "Constitutional Democracy and Social Welfare," *op. cit.*

13. See *Federalist Papers,* Nos. 45, 46. Note, however, Madison's arguments for preserving minority rights by transferring authority from the local to the national level in Papers 10 and 51. Also, we should note that following Dahl, *op. cit.*, we employ a "populistic democracy" model in this section where elections are thought of as expressions of voter preferences for public policies. In Section III where we discuss constitutional decisions, the implicit model of democracy will be closer to "Madisonian Democracy" where elections are viewed as the selection of "good" decision-makers. On this distinction see Kendall and Carey, *op. cit.*, 20-24.

14. The normatively disturbing interpersonal utility comparison problem inherent in the equal-stake condition may be removed by assuming boundaries are drawn and issues allocated at the constitutional stage by voters who assume they have an equal probability of assuming the position and tastes of other voters in future generations. The determination of the fiscal federalism questions so as to satisfy the equal-stake condition then becomes a necessary condition for maximizing the expected utility of the voter at the constitutional stage (which we will discuss in Section III). Also, see Mueller, "Fiscal Federalism in a Constitutional Democracy," *op. cit.*, for a discussion of this problem, and E. Haefele, "A Utility Theory of Representative Government," *American Economic Review,* 61 (July, 1971): 350–67, for a discussion of the importance of how issues are formulated and how the legislative agenda is drawn up to democratic decision-making.

15. See, for example, J. M. Buchanan and G. Tullock, *The Calculus of Consent* (Ann Arbor: University of Michigan Press, 1962); J. Coleman, "The Possibility of a Social Welfare Function," *American Economic Review,* 56 (December, 1966): 1105-22; and "Political Money," *American Political Science Review,* 64 (December, 1970): 1074-87; D. Mueller, "The Possibility of a Social Welfare Function: Comment," *American Economic Review,* 57 (December, 1967): 1304-11; and Parks, "The Possibility of a Social Welfare Function: Comment," *American Economic Review,* 57 (December, 1967): 1300-1304.

16. Dennis C. Mueller, Geoffrey C. Philpotts, and Jaroslav Vanek, "The Social Gains from Exchanging Votes: A Simulation Approach," *Public Choice,* 13 (Fall, 1972): 55–79. See also Robert Wilson, "An Axiomatic Model of Logrolling," *American Economic Review,* 59 (June, 1969): 331–41.

17. Coleman, "The Possibility of a Social Welfare Function." See

also "Comments" by Mueller and Parks and "Reply" by Coleman in *American Economic Review*, 57 (December, 1967): 1300–1317.

18. Note, however, the suggestion of James C. Miller, III, to take advantage of advances in communications technology and institute a national referendum. We reject the national referendum as a device for returning to direct democracy on the grounds that representation properly economizes information-gathering and the making of informed choices. See James C. Miller, III, "A Program for Direct and Proxy Voting in the Legislative Process," *Public Choice*, 7 (Fall, 1969): 107–13, and Martin Shubik, "On Homo Politicus and the Instant Referendum," *Public Choice*, 9 (Fall, 1970): 79–84. For a fuller discussion of the issues raised by Miller and Shubik, see our "Representative Democracy Via Random Selection," *Public Choice*, 12, (Spring, 1972): 59-68.

19. One problem with some of the experiments with at-large proportional representation (e.g., as practiced in New York City in the 1930's) is that representatives were not given votes in the legislature in proportion to the numbers of supporters they had. Thus, minority party representatives had equal strength with major party representatives, producing the potential for a "tyranny of the minority." We should also note that an early champion of a proportional voting system based on the Hare system and without point voting was John Stuart Mill. See Mill, *Considerations on Representative Government* (London: Parkinson and Bourn, 1861).

20. One way to approximate the correct difference in initial vote stocks would be to take existing differences in government budgets between urban and rural areas as evidence of the correct dispersion in vote stocks. This procedure would allow *equally weighted* voters a chance to decide which equal-stake issues they felt more strongly about (e.g., national versus local).

21. Rosseau proposed a similar system for choosing an executive in an "ideal" democracy. See *The Social Contract* (Amsterdam: M. M. Rey, 1762), Book IV, Chapter III, "Concerning Elections." Also see Dahl, *After the Revolution* (New Haven: Yale University Press, 1970), pp. 149–53. Democracy by lot also was practiced in Athenian Democracy. See Parkinson, *The Evolution of Political Thought* (New York: Houghton Mifflin, 1958), pp. 173–75. On the origins of representation by lot, see Fustel de Coulanges, *The Ancient City*, 1864. He writes:

It is surprising that modern historians represent the drawing of lots as an invention of the Athenian democracy. It was, on the contrary, in full rigor under the rule of the aristocracy (Plutarch, *Pericles*, 9), and appears to have been as old as the archonship itself. Nor is it a democratic procedure: we know, indeed, that even in the time of Lysias and of Demosthenes, the names of all the citizens were not put in the urn (Lysias, *Orat., de Invalido*, c. 13; *in Andocidem*, c. 4): for a still stronger reason was this true when the Eupatrids only, or the Pentakosiomedimni could be archons. Passages of Plato show clearly what idea the ancients had of the drawing of lots; the thought which caused it to be employed for magistrate-priests like the archons, or for senators charged with holy duties like the prytanes, was a religious idea, and not a notion of equality. It is worthy of remark, that when the democracy gained the upper hand, it reserved the selection by lot for the choice of archons, to whom it left no real power, and gave it up in the choice of strategi, who then had the true authority. So that there was drawing of lots of magistracies which dated from the aristocratic age, and election for those that dated from the age of democracy. (p. 183, fn. 13)

For a more complete discussion of the random selection proposal, see our "Representative Democracy Via Random Selection," *op. cit.*

22. See Pauly and Willett, "Two Concepts of Equity," *Social Science Quarterly* (forthcoming), for the general discussion of the concepts of *ex ante* and *ex post* equity. Also, as we noted before, where voting is costly and non-voting is a problem, election returns, even under point voting, may be unrepresentative. With these conditions it is an open question as to whether direct election of a proportional legislature or random selection gives a better articulation of underlying preferences. One alternative discussed previously would be to have public investment to lower the costs of voting via computer technology, requiring voting, or rewarding or penalizing voting through poll payments or poll taxes. Indeed, to the extent that the failure to vote is a reflection of a divergence between the private and social gains from democratic participation, the latter proposal would be appropriate. The advantage of random selection in this regard is that it offers a lower cost method of obtaining a reasonable approximation of preferences. On the general problem of voting and non-voting see Tollison and Willett, *op. cit.* Further, this problem is in part a question of how much society should invest in a government. And it is an implication of recent work on vote trading that a well-working government may embody great political gains from trade for democratic citizens, and hence, investments in reforming democratic process may have big pay-offs. See Mueller, Philpotts, and Vanek, "The Social Gains from Exchanging Votes," *op. cit.*

23. On this problem, which is endemic to democratic systems where voters directly elect legislators and which would also apply to our proposal for electing a proportionally representative body from an at-large list of candidates, see D. Black, *The Theory of Committees and Elections* (New York: Cambridge University Press, 1958), Chapter 11. Many of the operational details and the costs and benefits of the random procedure are discussed more fully in our "Representative Democracy Via Random Selection." We should clarify one problem with the random procedure—namely, how large it would have to be to reflect accurately the distribution of voter

preference—especially since Dahl argues (*After the Revolution*, p. 152)
that 500 or 600 at most is the number of people who could participate
effectively in a random legislature. This may or may not be the case,
depending on the amount of sampling error one is willing to tolerate
vis-a-vis the costs of a larger legislature and depending on how one
meshes the random body with the existing legislative process. Given
that there is no prior knowledge about the population proportion being
sampled for (50–50), a sample size of 500 would yield a 95 percent
chance that the value being estimated lies within a range equal to
the reported percentages, plus or minus an error of 4.9 percent.
Doubling the sample size to 1000 would yield a 95 percent chance
with a 3.6 percent error. So it is probably true that very accurate
samples of the voting populace would have to be large. However,
this does not mean that a large random legislature is not feasible or
cannot be effective. For example, such a representative body could
be meshed with the existing political process by making it a purely
advisory body, or one house of a bicameral legislature could be
designated primarily to respond to (i.e., vote on) rather than initiate
legislation. For such a body large size would not necessarily be a
constraint on its effectiveness.

24. See Officer and Willett, *The International Monetary System*
(New York: Prentice-Hall, 1967), and the references cited there.

25. See Braybrooke, *Three Tests for Democracy: Personal Rights,
Human Welfare and Collective Preference* (New York: Random House,
1968). In effect our model to this point in setting up the equal-stake
requirement, allocating issues to the correct level of government, and
giving voters in any polity an equal stock of votes, has established
the traditional form of *ex ante*, or before-the-fact, type of political
equality, although going beyond the usual one man—one vote form
of this type of equality. As noted earlier, however, it is still possible
that even with the above conditions of our model satisfied, there
can be *persistent* majorities and minorities over time. In such a case
one may wish to consider the imposition of a vote tax at the constitutional stage which would take away votes from abnormally high
winners and subsidize abnormally high losers in such a way as to
force everyone in the polity to win on average roughly the same
amount of the time. The vote-tax system would thus solve the long-
run form of the intensity problem where a majority persistently wins
on the issues in a given polity and establish political equality in an
ex post sense. This sort of vote-tax system would be very analogous
to handicapping systems in sports (e.g., golf). For a thorough
discussion of the concepts of *ex ante* and *ex post* quality and of the
resolution of long-run "tyranny of the majority" problems, see M. V.
Pauly and T. D. Willett, "Two Concepts of Equity," *op. cit.*, and
D. C. Mueller, R. D. Tollison and T. D. Willett, "On Equalizing the
Distribution of Political Income," *op. cit.*

26. This is consistent with the drift of Lowi's argument in *The End of Liberalism*.

27. Tullock stresses this difference in information possessed by the local voter in "A Simple Algebraic Logrolling Model," *American Economic Review*, LX (June, 1970): 419–26.

28. A classic example of this is the tariff protecting a geographically concentrated industry. Since a tariff typically benefits only a small minority and hurts everyone through higher prices, no single tariff can typically pass (unless part of a general logroll where, for example, a defense base is traded for a tariff) in the legislature. The Christmas Tree package of tariff legislation generated by Congress in 1970 in response to the President's support for tariff protection for one industry only (textiles) is an example of this point. Fortunately, none of the versions of the Christmas Tree bill reached the floor of the House and no trade legislation was raised during the session. A bill containing tariffs favoring a large number of geographically concentrated industries might pass, however. Such a bill would produce random and probably small changes in the distribution of income, and most likely leave society worse off on balance, by distorting world prices and relinquishing some of the gains from trade. Thus, the bill would be a negative-sum game in that some industries might increase their real incomes at the expense of others, and on the average real incomes in the nation would go down.

29. For examples of pro-logrolling arguments see Buchanan and Tullock, *The Calculus of Consent*; Coleman, "The Possibility of a Social Welfare Function," and "Political Money"; the various works of Robert Dahl; Arthur Bentley, *The Process of Government* (Bloomington: Principal Press, 1938) (first published 1908); and Madison's *Federalist Papers*. See Lowi, *The End of Liberalism*, and G. McConnell, *Private Power and American Democracy* (New York: Knopf, 1966), for anti-logrolling positions.

30. Again, it is interesting to note how John Stuart Mill recognized the importance of establishing a separate body (in his case a commission to select the issues upon which the legislature must act), *op. cit.*, pp. 235 ff.

31. For a discussion of convergence toward the center and instability in a multi-party system, see Melvin J. Hinich and Peter C. Ordeshook, "Plurality Maximization vs. Vote Maximization: A Spatial Analysis with Variable Participation," *American Political Science Review*, LXIV (September, 1970): 785–88.

32. Hinich and Ordeshook find that there can be as many as three conversion points for a unimodel distribution, if voters abstain from voting (due, for example, to alienation effects) as candidates move from their positions. *Ibid.*

33. Downs, *op. cit.*, pp. 122–27. Downs' book touches on a number of the issues raised in this paper about two-party and

multi-party systems. Also see Gordon Tullock, *Toward a Mathematics of Politics* (Ann Arbor: University of Michigan Press, 1967), Chapter X.

34. S. M. Lipset, *Political Man* (Garden City, N.Y.: Doubleday, 1960).

35. See in particular Lipset's discussion of the election of 1860 when there were four viable parties with presidential candidates, *ibid.*, Chapter 11.

36. For an empirical survey of the effect of parliamentary party structure on the stability of governments (1960 cases), see M. Taylor and V. M. Herman, "Party Systems and Government Stability," *American Political Science Review*, LXV (March, 1971): 28–37. This study finds that there is a strong relationship between stability of government and fragmentation of the parliamentary party system and of the government parties. No relation is found between fragmentation of opposition parties and stability. Also, the ideological disparity of parties did not seem to explain stability any better than a fragmentation stressing the number and size of parties. Interestingly, the proportion of seats held by "anti-system" (mainly, Communists and Neo-Fascists) parties did seem to be linked to stability.

Comments on
"Solving the Intensity Problem in Representative Democracy"

WILLIAM S. VICKREY[*]

Mueller, Tollison and Willett present us with some intriguing approaches to the perennially elusive goal of a method of achieving optimal social choices. However, I have to report that the attempt, like so many others, still falls short of a solution, though it does provide some suggestions well worth following up.

The basic problem is that any social-choice method that violates Arrow's independence requirement, as the instant methods clearly must, *ipso facto* become vulnerable to strategy. That is, the outcome may be influenced in favor of a given voter by variations in his voting procedure motivated by what he thinks the behavior of the others is likely to be, rather than by sole attention to his own personal preferences. This can range from deliberate falsification of the reporting of preferences, as in schemes where a number of alternatives are to be ranked, to the concentration of votes on issues thought to be close decisions, as in multiple-voting schemes.

Vulnerability to strategy may, indeed, not be a fatal defect in all cases. On the one hand, we are shown in the Von Neumann-Morgenstern version of game theory that if all participants are sophisticated and negotiation costs are nil, all stable outcomes must be efficient in the Pareto sense,

[*] Professor of Economics, Columbia University.

i.e., not admitting any change within the set of alternatives that are attainable within the constraints that have been imposed that will benefit some without hurting others. Unfortunately, the degree of sophistication required is such that all the participants would have to know more about game theory than Von Neumann and Morgenstern put together, and would have to have greater skill at combinations than Fischer and Spassky combined! Moreover, in spite of the magnificent technological advances in the art of communication we have seen recently, even minor negotiation costs critically impair this result. Thus, the solution that Coase and others of the Chicago school at times seem to be proposing, that we simply define with great accuracy all property rights from rights to pollute or to enjoy clean air to rights not to be offended by pornographic displays, graffiti, or billboards, simply is not available or even approachable to any satisfactory degree.

On the other hand, vulnerability to strategy may not be a fatal defect if nobody in fact behaves strategically, whether out of ignorance or out of conscientious scruple. Our authors seem to assume that in a multiple-voting scheme voters will allocate their votes according to the intensity of their preferences over the various issues, without regard to their feelings as to the likelihood that their votes will be decisive. If this is in fact the case, then conceivably some kind of stable and hopefully close to optimal result may indeed emerge. And to be sure, if the number of voters is large and the issues clearly independent, a naive electorate might behave in approximately this way. But in this day of polling, one could expect that pollsters would be more than ever on the job attempting to determine which issues are in fact close and to inform the electorate of their findings. Complaints that polls influence the outcome would have more substance than ever, in spite of the fact that because of the heightened strategic interaction between poll results and actual outcomes, the polls might become more inaccurate than ever.

To make the system even approximately viable one might have to prohibit polling, at least with respect to election issues; but even so it would be hard to prevent pundits from expressing their judgments concerning the political situation, possibly with even less predictable results if the pundits are either prejudiced or themselves resort to strategical bias in their reports, deliberately or otherwise.

There remains the possibility that voters might conscientiously reflect their preferences. Indeed, in small, closely linked groups where a degree of personal acquaintance and interaction exists, this becomes a real possibility; and in a meeting where exchange of views can take place freely, there is a real possibility that, as in a Quaker meeting, a consensus is reached that a given outcome may be the best for the group, even where this is admittedly contrary to the individual preferences of some. In most political jurisdictions, however, this degree of harmony is still far out of reach.

Direct voting on issues, while conceptually simple, in practice tends to confuse voters unless the issues are strictly limited in number, so that we are driven to decision-making by representatives. Representation by random sample is an attractive idea, in the abstract: it, however, implies a less expert body of decision-makers than would in principle be attainable through some other mode of selection. One might, indeed, consider a two-body legislature in which a random panel or jury would make decisions regarding broad issues for which no expertise would be needed (if there are any such), while a "senate" of experts would deal with the most involved issues. But one is led to wonder whether the issues to be determined by the random assembly would not turn out to be an empty set.

If a representative body is to be elected, the proposals discussed by our authors are suggestive, but somewhat inconclusive. The notion that representatives might be accorded a voting power in their representative capacity proportional to the number of votes they garner has some appeal. It is not quite clear from the paper just what this mechanism is to be. There is reference to a "primary," which as I see it would have to differ from existing primaries in that the individuals to be given seats in the representative body would be definitively selected, and a "secondary" (??) in which the electorate would in effect decide to which of these representatives they would give their proxy, presumably that representative with whose general position they felt the greatest affinity. But here again, there is a conflict between giving weight to issues that are considered most important to the individual and issues where he feels the award of his proxy has the greatest chance of being of importance.

Strategy enters in another way also, as the aspiring representatives may present their position not in terms of their own independently arrived at judgments, but in terms of what they feel will give them a better chance of appealing to the electorate, first for a seat in the assembly, and then for a larger share of the proxies. Here I think the authors rather overstate the tendency of positions to converge to the middle, at least in terms of the one-dimensional model they present. In the models presented some years ago by Lerner and Singer, stable situations of sorts were obtained on the assumption that customers were distributed at uniform density along a market, where an even number of sellers would be distributed in pairs in such a way as to divide the market up evenly, though not efficiently. In a multi-dimensional setting it is not clear that any equilibrium emerges or whether it would have any desirable properties.

The procedure is not completely specified, especially as to how the "primary" is to be run. One might imagine a voting scheme of electing a fixed number of candidates from a field initially open or determined by modest qualification requirements. But whether a single final vote, or multiple voting, or Hare-transferable voting, or multiple transferable voting is used, strategic elements will exist; and there is no guarantee that the successful candidates will span a satisfactorily wide range of positions. Given the membership of the assembly, each voter would then in the final election give his proxy to that member whose overall position is in some sense closest to his own. One can speculate whether there would be any gains in allowing the proxy to be subdivided among several members. Again, strategy is not obviously unprofitable to the knowledgeable individual, even though the theorem that a Nash equilibrium point is sure to exist given certain prerequisites could be held to indicate the contrary.

Under these circumstances, what is the optimal method of selecting the membership of the assembly? Without more analysis it would be rash for me to say, but my instinct (or perhaps merely prejudice) is that some elements of the Hare-transferable vote would be needed. And in this day of computers, the mechanical difficulties associated with the Hare system, where paper ballots are handled, is no longer a problem.

At another level, one may ask whether a system in which members of an assembly have voting power in proportion to the number they represent is desirable. The member with the highest voting power is likely to wield an influence considerably, but indefinably greater than members with an equal aggregate number of proxies. For this reason one might argue against any wide dispersion of voting power. One way of doing this would be to have the seat of any one attracting an unduly large number of proxies split into two or more.

4

Anarchy as a Norm of Social Choice

ROGER A. MCCAIN[*]

To speak of anarchy as a norm of anything seems paradoxical. Anarchy suggests chaos, the absence of norms.
According to Malatesta, however, this suggestion is "owing
to the prejudice that . . . a society without government must
be given up to disorder, and oscillate between the unbridled
dominion of some and the blind vengeance of others."[1] Since
anarchists have not accepted that "prejudice" there is no
inconsistency in seeking in their ideas a norm of social choice.

Anarchism is a tendency which occurs in a variety of
social movements. In the nineteenth century European socialism, Republicanism, and syndicalism generated "no-govern-
ment" factions. The Russian "terrorist" party had its anarchist
offshoot, which leaves us the stereotype of the anarchist as
assassin. These anarchist factions, despite their disparate
roots, mingle in an anarchist social movement in Europe,
which was strongest, before Fascism, in the Latin countries
of Europe and America. In the United States the abolitionist
movement, utopian socialism, and other influences nourished
a native, individualist anarchism.

In Europe anarchism was often the ideology of the urban-
ized peasant (Proudhon), the miner, the craftsman (the
watchmakers of the Swiss Jura), the artist, the landless rural
worker, sometimes the bandit. These groups spoke not for

---

[*] Assistant Professor, Western Washington State College; the author is
now Assistant Professor of Economics, The City College of the City
University of New York.

the working class or the peasant class as a whole, but for special minorities—deviant, despised, or especially cohesive, rural people, or people with their roots in the country, people crushed under the sheer mass of modern mass society. Majority rule would offer them little hope; property-centered liberal society less. The anarchists conceived of a society which would be a union of special minorities, of localities and regions, no one predominating over another, and ideally of special people, no one predominating over another, "a generation of Princes"[2] in Woodcock's phrase. In this advocacy they developed a kind of social theory, mostly tacit and implicit in the "utopian" and revolutionary proposals of the anarchists.

By "tacit social theory" I mean a consistent and distinctive set of principles underlying the propaganda and "utopian" or post-revolutionary proposals of a particular social movement. Of course, there may be no such principles. However, the investigator of anarchism faces a particular difficulty in assessing the consistency of anarchist principles. The difficulty is that ordinary language is hopelessly ambiguous, from the anarchist viewpoint. Malatesta's "prejudice" is a case in point. As a result, anarchists often introduce novel terminology or novel definitions of words in common usage. Much of Proudhon's reputation as a "man of paradox"[3] stems from his ironic playing on what he evidently considered to be the ambiguity of common language.[4] Thus we find that Malatesta describes anarchy as a condition of society without constituted authority,[5] while Giovanni Baldelli describes it as "The Rule of Authority."[6] Perhaps somewhat distinct from this, we have to contend with a Buddhist-like "no-sense" in anarchist thought.[7]

This essay will concentrate mainly on the collectivist tradition of anarchism—the tradition of Proudhon, Bakunin, and Kropotkin, and of Emma Goldman, Malatesta, and Martin Buber. Religious anarchism, pacifist and individualist anarchism are neglected in part because there is a greater

consistency within the collectivist tradition than there is
among the four different branches. Among the collectivists,
at least, there is no opposition to organization *per se*. The
future society is conceived of as a network of voluntary
organizations of particular kinds. It is often specified that
the organizations should be cooperative in nature, and in
some sense democratic. Worker self-management is a consistent anarchist demand. "Democracy" means direct democracy; representative institutions are greatly distrusted at
best, and commonly rejected. There is in this at least some
recognition that some kinds of decisions are inherently social[8]
and, indeed, the collectivist anarchists would agree with
socialism in viewing as social many decisions which conservatives would view as private. (Here individualists would
be likely to agree with the conservatives.)

In this quick sketch, and more especially in the more
detailed and various proposals of Bakunin, Kropotkin, and
the rest there is, I think, a theory of social choice. The theory
is partly normative and partly positive, as one might expect.
It is based on three principles: free agreement (normative),
the "iron law of oligarchy"[9] (positive), and the incompetence
of laws (positive). The three principles are, however,
interdependent.

The anarchist demand is for liberty for each individual
and each group. This raises the question of how conflicts
between different persons/groups are to be resolved. It is
here that the anarchist parts company from the nineteenth-
century liberal. For the anarchist, these conflicts are to be
settled not by law, but by "free agreement."[10] This is a
vague term but perhaps no more vague than the rest of
the political lexicon. For now, it will be enough to observe
that agreements are *not* free when the threat of violence
or overwhelming force plays a part in determining the agreement. To avoid some possible confusion, and to illustrate
that free agreement is a radical norm, let us in passing
notice the implication of free agreement for certain kinds

of property institutions. In particular, consider the relationship of landlord and tenant. It may appear that in promising to pay rent for the use of land, the tenant has entered into a free agreement. Why, however, has the tenant agreed to pay for the use of land? Because he has little, and the landlord has much. Thus the landlord-tenant agreement could not exist but for a particular *distribution* of property, which could hardly be maintained against squatting and encroachment except by the threat of violence or overwhelming force.[11] It is not a free agreement, for the norm does not say "the *direct* threat of violence" or "the threat of violence unless the threat is made under the cover of a property right."

The "iron law of oligarchy" of Michels holds that large organizations are inevitably ruled by small cliques at the top, regardless of "democratic" ideology or intent. This is clearly an empirical or historical judgment. Following Olson,[12] we may consider the "iron law" as a corollary of a more general proposition about the costs of coordinating action in small and large groups. Olson's hypothesis is that the costs of coordination are prohibitive in the case of large groups, with the paradoxical-seeming result that large groups are relatively impotent. The impotence of the masses to control mass organizations is then a case in point.

The "incompetence of the law" is an attitude that the reality of human interaction is so complex that no code of laws can really effectively determine the relations among people. Rather, the laws will have to be interpreted, and the law becomes whatever the judges say it is. ". . . the fecundity of the unexpected far outstrips any foresight on the part of the statesman, and more legislation only gives rise to more litigation. This requires of those in power both initiative and powers of arbitration. . . ."[13] The hypothesis of the incompetence of law is one which the anarchists share (improbably as it may seem) with monarchists, twentieth-century liberals, and other believers in a strong "executive" power. It implies a rejection of the nineteenth-century liberal's reliance on a set of automatic rules, in the same way that the twentieth-century liberal's stress on "flexibility" does. It also implies a rejection of the distinction between a "constitutional stage" of public choice and a post-constitutional stage, a distinction which has been stressed by such public-choice theorists as Buchanan and Tullock[14] and Mueller.[15] Notwithstanding, their ideas and reasoning can be reinterpreted, and shed some light on the anarchist-collectivist program.[16] I will return to this below.

Let us now explore the implications of this system of values and hypotheses, to see what sort of institutions it suggests.

1. Clearly, all organizations in an anarchist society must be voluntary organizations. This follows directly from the principle of "free agreement." Whenever the liberty of an individual and a group conflict, the difference must be settled by free agreement; that would not be so if the organization were mandatory. The state is not a voluntary organization, of course—no anarchist would agree that it is[17]—even though it is surely possible for a person to leave the country he was born in. "Love it or leave it" is not enough. That way lies a whole nest of paradoxes.

To use Hirschman's terminology, a voluntary organization is one in which "exit" is possible and the *price for exit* is low.[18] Thus it is not only permissible for a person to dissociate himself from the organization, but also practical. This will often mean that there should be more than one organization performing a particular function, so that the exiter can reaffiliate himself with another group,[19] thus limiting the cost of exit. Organizations should therefore be as small as feasible, and must have no "constituted authority" which would enable them to impose artificial penalties for exit.

The "iron law of oligarchy" also reinforces this bias for small organizations, both positively and negatively. It supports smallness positively in that an organization *which is* a small group will be more effective in meeting the needs of its members, because better controlled by them. More important, perhaps, is the negative support the "iron law" gives to smallness and exit as means of control. The alternative to exit is voice. What the "iron law" says is that voice is not effective for the mass membership of a large organization,[20] so that exit, or smallness, or both, are so much more important. The "incompetence of law" offers further negative support, since we cannot expect any overriding constitutional or legal order to require organizations to be responsive to voice. Thus, only the threat of exit will in fact make the organizations responsive to voice.[21]

2. Free agreement also supports smallness and multiplicity of organizations by another chain of reasoning. Within a larger organization conflicts of purpose or of liberty among subgroups are more likely than would be the case in a smaller organization. Such conflicts must be resolved by free agreement, not by the dominance of one group over another. This seems to mean that wherever possible, subgroups have the right to secede from the larger organizations. Thus large organizations must be confederations of smaller organizations.[22]

We may illustrate these principles by reference to Kropotkin's speculations about the organization of economic activity "on the morrow of the social revolution." Local economic organization is expected to be voluntary and communistic: "Take, for example, an association stipulating that each of its members should carry out the following contract: 'We undertake to give you the use of our houses, stores, streets, means of transport schools, museums, etc., on condition that, from twenty to forty-five or fifty years of age, you consecrate four or five hours a day to some work recognized as necessary to existence. . . . And, finally, if it does not please you, . . . seek adherents and organize with them on novel principles.' "[23] "Today, when groups scattered far and wide wish to organize themselves for some object or other, . . . Where it is not possible to meet directly or come to agreement by correspondence, delegates versed in the question at issue are sent, and they are told, 'Endeavor to come to an agreement on such or such a question, and then return, not with a law in your pocket, but with a proposition of agreement which we may or may not accept.' "[24]

3. "Majority rule" is clearly inadmissible under the norm of free agreement. If the majority and the minority disagree, then their differences should be settled by free agreement, not by the rule of either group over the other. This does not, however, exclude taking collective decisions by majority voting. *Within the context* of voluntary, decentralized organizations of the kind outlined under 1. and 2. above, collective decisions might be taken by majority voting, either of the whole group or of representatives.

On this possibility anarchists have no consensus; but this lack of consensus may itself be revealing about anarchist principles. Morris' acceptance of majority *rule* but not enforcement[25] would be followed by many anarchists. Baldelli's version of majority rule subject to equality of sacrifice[26] is less common, actually. Many anarchists support workers' councils, a species of representative majoritarian institution, but others criticize them[27] in favor of direct workers' assemblies. At the other end of the scale we have Emma Goldman's contempt for majorities,[28] which seems to imply an equal contempt for majority voting.

As Buchanan and Tullock observe, there would be no reason for any departure from unanimity rule if there were no cost of making decisions.[29] When there are costs of making decisions unanimously, an individual may rationally prefer a less costly means of decision-making despite the expectation that some decisions would go against her or his interests. In the scheme of Buchanan and Tullock, these preferences are expressed in choosing a constitution. To an anarchist, this is feckless, since a constitution, being a form of law, settles nothing. However, in a system of voluntary organizations, these preferences could be expressed by remaining in "democratic" organizations instead of shifting to otherwise similar "consensual" ones. The range of opinion on the role of "democratic" decision mechanisms within voluntary organizations may well reflect a similar range of opinion on the costs of making unanimous decisions.

4. This analysis might be ramified in several ways. Trial by jury bears interpretation in terms of free agreement,[30] as does a preference for the *Lex Terrae*,[31] customary law,[32] over formal legislation. Still other expressions of free agreement and *mutualité* might be found and analyzed, but instead we proceed along the lines of the previous paragraph.

On its face, "free agreement" seems to be a form of unanimity rule, and, indeed, R. P. Wolff has argued "In Defense of Anarchism,"[33] that "unanimous direct democracy" is a system of society which is consistent with individual moral responsibility,[34] i.e., his concept on anarchy. On the other hand, I have just been arguing that free agreement is not necessarily or exactly a system of unanimity rule, just as an idealized democratic constitution, in force through unanimous choice is not necessarily or exactly a system of unanimity rule. Each might approach unanimity rule, in the limit, depending upon the decisions made by the constitution-choosers or the organization-choosers in the two systems, respectively.

Still, it seems likely that the system of voluntary, decentralized and confederated organizations advocated by the collectivist anarchists would come nearer to unanimity rule, in practice, than most extant constitutional systems would even if they worked ideally (i.e., if the "iron law of oligarchy" and the "incompetence of law" did not interfere with the working of constitutional systems as advertised).

Buchanan and Tullock observe[35] that the costs of unanimous decision-making vary with the nature of the institutional system. It seems clear that the confederative-consultative set-up would make for a low cost of unanimous decision-making. That is, the alternative cost of unanimous decision-making, over and above the cost of simply maintaining the confederative-consultative system, would be relatively small. The reference here is to the communication cost of decision-making. Buchanan and Tullock also stress[36] costs incident on strategic bargaining. We might speculate that this cost would also be lower under free agreement, since one person would not in general be able to frustrate collective action. (I will return to this point below.) Further, the relative ease of generating consensus may be increased, in a decentralized system, by a process of circular cumulative causation *a la* Myrdal. It is argued that mobility increases homogeneity at the local level, while also increasing diversity among localities, thus further encouraging mobility.[37] (An implicit assumption here is, seemingly, that consensus is harder to achieve within than among local communities, other things begin equal. Some might object that this is so only in a class society.) Finally, there may be some tendency toward consensus rather than simple majority rule in "town-meeting" democracy.[38]

As noted, there is at least one major point of distinction between the "unanimity rule" visualized by Buchanan and Tullock and that which free agreement tends toward in the extreme. It is a difference as to what is to be *decided* by unanimity rule. For Buchanan and Tullock, unanimity is supposed to be a prerequisite for any collective action. By collective action Buchanan and Tullock mean any action which imposes costs on more than one person.[39] Under free agreement, it is not action but restraint which does not take place except on the basis of unanimity. Clearly this leads to a different result. To confound the matter a little further, we might recall "The Impossibility of a Paretian Liberal."[40]

The Pareto rule is yet another species of unanimity rule and, again, it differs from both Buchanan-and-Tullock unanimity and free agreement in that it is a different class of decisions which require unanimity—departures from the *status quo*. Buchanan and Tullock and other constitutionalists evade the Paretian-Liberal problem by reserving unanimous decision to a (hypothetical) unanimous choice of a constitution, within which decisions may well be non-Paretian. Free agreement evades the same problem by a simple presumption against restraint.[41] (This seems to be Wolff's intention with respect to "unanimous direct democracy," but that is not perfectly clear.)

What these contrasts strongly suggest is that we ought to beware of references to unanimity rule as though it were a single system. The outcome of a system of unanimity rule depends on the state of society which is realized in the absence of agreement. Without committing ourselves to the equation of "unanimity rule" and bargaining,[42] we may illustrate this by reference to a classical bargaining theory. Figure 1 is a standard Edgeworth box. Depending

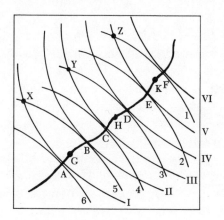

FIGURE 1

on whether the initial allocation is X, Y, or Z, the outcome of bargaining must be along the contract curve in segments AB, CD, and EF, respectively. Even if some post-classical theory of bargaining should narrow the range of possible outcomes, as to G, H, and K, respectively, they must clearly still be distinct, depending on the initial allocation.

We might think of a particular scheme of unanimity rule as a sort of normative social contract theory. The social contract theorists held that government had (in effect) been accepted as a purely voluntary contract in order to obtain the advantages of civil society relative to the natural state of society. The constitutionalist ideal is a normative social contract theory in an obvious sense. The ideas of Buchanan and Tullock clearly visualize as the "natural state of society" (i.e., the normative alternative) a system without collective action. This seems a reasonable interpretation of the contractarian "natural state" until we reflect that for Buchanan and Tullock, no collective action entails no external costs. Indeed, external costs seem to be a feature of the contractarian "natural state," and one which the civil society is designed to limit.

Nevertheless the two cases are parallel. The "natural state of society" is determined, not by nature in fact, but by the logic of the particular matter to be determined by unanimity. The hypothetical framers of the social contract were negotiating not collective action but collective restraint (like the anarchists), and more particularly legal restraint (unlike the anarchists). This parallel should not be surprising since anarchist theory evolved from contractarian theory, especially in Godwin's writings.[43]

One other point should be dealt with before concluding, and it is the obvious *prima facie* objection to any scheme for a society based on purely voluntary organizations. The objection is that such a society would not supply public services or "collective goods" adequately. (I do not say that a voluntary society would fail to provide optimum quantities of collective goods because that would suggest that a society of some other sort would supply optimum quantities of public goods, a very doubtful point at best.) It is indeed clear that under free agreement, some people would be able to act as free riders, and presumably would do so.

Few anarchists have spoken to this point, unfortunately.[44] The ultimate anarchist response to this criticism could, I believe, only be a negative one, which would parallel an argument for free trade against the nationalistic "optimum tariff." The argument for free trade first grants that a positive tariff would be optimal, but proceeds to assert that the tariff which would come forth from an imperfect political process would not be optimum but would depart from the optimum in such a systematic way as to be worse than free trade, even from a nationalist viewpoint. Indeed, the free trader might refer to the "iron law of oligarchy" or to Olson's group theory to support the point. It seems that the anarchist could clearly make a similar argument, in the much broader context of public goods in general. However, this is an argument from the lesser evil, and many anarchists would not accept any such argument.

Olson, having pointed out that a collective organization is a collective good, goes on to observe that it is a fallacy to suppose that organizations will spring up spontaneously. He refers to it as "the anarchist fallacy."[45] It seems to me that Olson is being somewhat unfair to the anarchists, here. One cannot deny Peter Kropotkin's sunny optimism, quoted,[46] about spontaneous organization "on the morrow of the social revolution"; but a case can be made that anarchist-collectivists have held a "by-product" theory of organization. This seems to me to be the upshot of Bakunin's "living unity" (i.e., based on economic interests) in a libertarian society and the "artificial" political unity, in the passage quoted by Olson.[47] A similar, and much more explicit, comment has been made by an influential present-day anarchist.[48] Anyway, vague as the by-product theory has been, even if present, there is another strand in collectivist-anarchist ideas which is quite explicit and which meets the objection with regard to public goods, at least in part. All anarchists have proposed to make large organization federations, "from the bottom up," of autonomous small organizations. This policy Olson explicitly admits[49] as an exception to his general rule about the incompetence of large groups. Thus, with extensive reliance on federative organization and "public opinion" within small groups, an anarchist society might not be in a very bad way for public goods and services.

My conclusion is, quite simply, that anarchist ideas deserve to be taken more seriously by scholars than they typically have been. There is, admittedly, much chaff in the anarchist wheat (as there also is, no doubt, in the conservative barley, the socialist oats, and the liberal corn). The ideal of "free agreement" seems a quite real and valuable approach to social choice, which offers some insights by way of contrast on both the constitutionalist school and the several varieties of economic *etatism* which one encounters in welfare economics and social choice theory. We ought not limit our critical attention to those social doctrines which have already conquered society in some region, or come close to it. Speculation and even fiction, especially utopian fiction, has a profound effect on human consciousness.[50] So it should. The human mind is not limited by the reality of the present, and the future is always a surprise.

NOTES

1. Errico Malatesta, *Anarchy* (London: Freedom Press, 1942), p. 7.

2. George Woodcock, *Anarchism* (New York: World, 1962), p. 34.

3. *Ibid.*, p. 106.

4. Compare Charles Rosen's comment on Proudhon in "Romantics," *New York Review of Books*, XX, No. 10 (June 14, 1973), p. 16.

5. Malatesta, *loc. cit.*

6. Giovanni Baldelli, *Social Anarchism* (Harmondsworth, Middlesex, England: Penguin Books, Inc., 1971), Ch. 5.

7. Rudolf deJong, "Provos and Kabouters," in D. E. Apter and James Joll, *Anarchism Today* (Garden City, N.Y.: Doubleday, 1972), p. 193.

8. See William Morris, *News from Nowhere, The Collected Works of William Morris,* XVI (London: Longmans, Green, 1912), pp. 87–90, especially p. 90, for an interesting hypothetical example of majority rule *without* enforcement in an "inherently social" decision.

9. Cited in A. O. Hirschman, *Exit, Voice and Loyalty* (Cambridge, Mass.: Harvard University Press, 1970), p. 84. Compare P. Kropotkin, *The Conquest of Bread* (New York: Blom, 1913 and 1968), p. 215.

10. The term is taken from Kropotkin, *op. cit.*; however, Kropotkin's examples in *The Conquest of Bread* focus largely on the operation of free agreement in the present society.

11. "Violence" and "overwhelming force" are deeper concepts, in a philosophic sense, than they appear on the surface. See *Nomos XIV, Coercion* (Chicago: Aldine Atherton, 1972), for some examples. Note also Baldelli, *op. cit.*, p. 137.

12. M. Olson, *The Logic of Collective Action* (New York: Schocken, 1968).

13. Stewart Edwards, ed., *Selected Writings of P. J. Proudhon* (Garden City, N.Y.: Doubleday Anchor Books, 1969), p. 104.

14. J. M. Buchanan and G. Tullock, *The Calculus of Consent* (Ann Arbor: University of Michigan Press, 1965).

15. D. Mueller, "Constitutional Democracy and Social Welfare," *Quart. J. Econ.*, LXXXVII (Feb., 1973), 60–80.

16. I have not seen G. Tullock, *Explorations in the Theory of Anarchy* (Blacksburg, Va.: Center for the Study of Public Choice, 1972).

17. G. Tullock has given a clear rebuttal of the proposition that people get "the kind of government they deserve" in his economic analysis of revolutionary activism. See "The Paradox of Revolution," *Public Choice*, XI (Fall, 1971): 89–100. Tullock does not distinguish between revolutions and *coups d'etat*, but if we make that distinction in an obvious way, Tullock's point is that revolutions are rare indeed, by comparison with *coups d'etat*.

18. Hirschman, *op. cit.*, note 9 above. See pp. 76, 96–97.

19. Judith Hicks Stiehm has proposed a scheme of legislation which would have this characteristic. From an anarchist viewpoint that proposal is "utopian," as is any legalistic reform, in that it overlooks the incompetence of law. *Nonviolent Power* (Lexington, Mass.: Heath, 1972), pp. 75, 75n, 107. The discussion of this paragraph owes a great deal to Paul Goodman, *People or Personnel* (New York: Vintage Books, 1968). See also Baldelli, *op. cit.*, p. 82.

20. Hirschman, *op. cit.*, p. 84.

21. *Ibid.*, p. 82.

22. *Ibid.*, p. 86. See also *News from Nowhere* (periodical, pub. Edmonton, Alta., Can.), vol. 2, no. 2, p. 12.

23. Kropotkin, *op. cit.*, pp. 206–207.

24. *Ibid.*, p. 46; also Baldelli, *op. cit.*, pp. 120, 141.

25. See note 8.

26. Baldelli, *op. cit.*, p. 104.

27. M. Bookchin, *Post-Scarcity Anarchism* (Berkeley: The *Ramparts* Press, 1971), pp. 145–47.

28. Emma Goldman, *Anarchism* (New York: Dover, 1969), pp. 69–78.

29. Buchanan and Tullock, *op. cit.*, Ch. 7.

30. Lysander Spooner, an American individualist anarchist, has so interpreted trial by jury. See *An Essay on the Trial by Jury* (New York: Da Capo Press, 1971).

31. *Ibid.*

32. Baldelli, *op. cit.*, p. 55.

33. R. P. Wolff, *In Defense of Anarchism* (New York: Harper Torch Books, 1970).

34. But compare W. L. McBride, "Voluntary Association: The Basis of an Ideal Model, and the 'Democratic' Failure," in *Nomos XI, Voluntary Associations* (New York: Atherton, 1969), pp. 202–32; also S. T. Glass, *The Responsible Society: The Ideas of the English Guild Socialists* (London: Longmans, Green, 1966).

35. Buchanan and Tullock, *op. cit.*, pp. 76–77.

36. *Ibid.*, pp. 98–99.

37. This roughly follows Goodman, *op. cit.*, note 19.

38. Jane J. Mansbridge, "Town Meeting Democracy," in *Working Papers*, 1, no. 2 (Summer, 1973). See esp. p. 9, and references cited there. In Mansbridge's example, consensus is the tendency among those who live in the central village and thus participate in its "culture of gossip," not in the entire township. This might be less of a problem within a voluntary organization.

39. While a scholar may define terms in whatever way she or he finds convenient, for analytical purposes, it is worth remarking that Buchanan and Tullock depart rather far from ordinary language in this. We might ordinarily say that an individual action (say, cooking barbecue) would impose costs (smoke) on others, which the others might well bear *passively*. We would normally consider this a *collective* action only if the neighbors joined in the picnic. For Buchanan and Tullock, it is a collective action even if only one person is "actively" engaged in it.

40. A. K. Sen, "The Impossibility of a Paretian Liberal," *J. Polit. Econ.* 78 (Jan./Feb., 1970), pp. 152–57.

41. I am indebted to Jim Bumpas, of Palo Alto, for alerting me to the importance of this point.

42. Bargaining *strictu sensu* begins with given alternatives and given tastes. Within unanimity rule, persuasion may change tastes and "creative bargaining" may lead to the discovery of new alternatives, preferred by both or all parties. I am indebted to Michael Mischaikow, Western Washington State College, for this latter point.

43. This follows April Carter, *The Political Theory of Anarchism* (New York: Harper Torchbooks, 1971), pp. 15–20.

44. The modern individualist "anarcho-capitalist," Murray Roth-bard, explicitly denies the possibility of any public-goods inter-dependencies; see H. E. Preche, "The Public Choice Theory of Murray N. Rothbard, a Modern Anarchist," *Public Choice*, 14 (Spring, 1973), pp. 143–54. This position seems implicit in the ideas of some other individualists as well. However, this is a major point of distinction between individualist and collectivist anarchists.

45. Olson, *op. cit.*, pp. 130–31.

46. *Ibid.*, p. 130.

47. *Ibid.*

48. Bookchin, *op. cit.*, p. 136, for example.

49. Olson, *op. cit.*, pp. 62-63.

50. It is worth recalling that state socialism had its roots in an utopian fiction, Etienne Cabet's *Voyage en Icarie*.

Comments on
"Anarchy as a Norm of Social Choice"

EDWIN P. REUBENS[*]

These comments begin with some general points about public-choice theory, and then apply them to McCain's paper on anarchism. There are four such general points concerning the so-called "new economics of public choice": (a) it is not quite "new"; (b) it is not fully representative of "economics"; (c) it is not fully "public" (in the operational sense of "social"); and (d) the theory is excessively restricted to "choice" in a rationalistic and rather mechanical sense.

Despite these carping remarks, I mean to praise the main body of the doctrine, not to bury it. For no one should neglect the genuine contributions of contemporary public-choice theory—notably its explorations of externalities, its attention to the increasing costs of information and agreement, and more basically its reexamination of social consent.

In making these contributions, our theorists are not really breaking new ground. Mostly they are re-plowing, more finely and more deeply, the terrain already broken and furrowed by Rousseau and other *philosophes* of eighteenth-century France and a long line of social philosophers in England and America, not to mention Socrates and Aristotle, let alone Pareto and John Rawls in our own time.

On the other hand, economists today seem to be innovating in bringing to choice analysis certain neat economic tools—

[*] Professor of Economics, The City College of the City University of New York.

such as the indifference curve, the social-utility function, and the unit-cost curve with its falling and rising stretches. Likewise the economists bring a strong insistence upon exact quantitative measurement—as in rate-of-return analysis, and benefit/cost calculations and comparisons. The trouble is that the economists also bring, often unawares, certain long-standing assumptions and models—particularly those relating to the behavior of *individuals*—which may or may not fit the subject matter of *social* behavior.

Probably the most important of these long-standing predispositions in methodology is the model of atomistic individualism. Many, perhaps most, economists are accustomed to think chiefly in terms of market models, in which each individual comes bearing his preference schedules, for the function of "interacting" with other such individuals, so as to "arrive at a consensus" in terms of establishing prices and the corresponding quantities. When economists apply this mechanism to social choice, they usually do not recognize how static and mechanical it is to postulate pre-fabricated individuals who, like a robot or a computer, are already programmed in their preferences, and need only work out their specific trade-offs among the already fixed "available opportunities."

Yet some economists have lately learned to complement individualistic micro-economics with macro-treatments, wherein the whole behaves rather differently from the mere sum of atomistic parts. Some economists have also learned to complement static equilibrium analysis with dynamic growth analyses and the assessment of historical processes. But as yet very few economists are prepared to come to grips with non-atomistic models which incorporate the social conditioning of the individual, the role of authority in situations of conflicting goals or identity crises, and the very basic process of learning-by-doing in the economic market, let alone socialization in the larger "market" of family and social relationships.

It would be a pity if the contemporary explorations of social choice were confined to the traditional individualism of micro-economics, just when modern social thought is grappling with the dynamic and interactive social processes which actually determine public choice. It would be a pity if we contented ourselves with speculative and largely introspective treatises on public choice, instead of going on to empirical studies of social behavior in the real world. If we want to understand, and perhaps to alter, the expansion and contraction of, say NASA, or the Model Cities program, or Medicaid, or local school financing, or mass transit versus the automobile, or the stockpiling of food in one country or in a new international agency, or any other public issue—we can, of course, learn a good deal from estimates of the benefit/cost ratios for the various alternatives; but also we must study the social, political and economic processes in which the decisions on these matters were enmeshed, and will always be enmeshed.

These general points may help to illuminate McCain's paper on anarchism. Evidently the current revival of anarchism responds to some deep-lying concerns today: the dissatisfactions and frustrations of modern life, the rebellions of youth against authority, the revolt of minorities against majorities, the efforts of individuals to escape from an increasingly tight society. To all these persons, with these often-inchoate feelings, philosophical anarchism offers an alternative way of thinking and feeling, and perhaps an alternative way of behaving. Witness the sudden, if short, vogue of Paul Goodman a decade ago, and more recently Charles Reich, and currently the spreading vogue of John Rawls with his libertarian theory of justice.

McCain has made a noble effort, carried out with thoughtfulness and sensitivity, to elucidate the social theory, or "theory of social choice," that is more or less implicit in the classic anarchist writings. The normative principle which he found is essentially the rule of "free agreement" (since the other two doctrines which he cites—"the iron law of oligarchy" and "the incompetence of the laws"—are empirical assertions, not normative principles, in my opinion).

Thus the anarchist writers, fanatically obsessed with the ideal of equality, insisted upon unanimous decision on every public issue. After full discussion of each issue, no matter what the costs of information and debate, if perfect agreement still could not be reached, the anarchists' ultimate resolution is for the dissenters to withdraw from the group. In this way, an absolute devotion to the sanctity of the individual ends in the dissolution of society at any moment! It is an attitude which may be called either heroic or quixotic, according to taste; but its social implication is clearly "anarchy" (this is the term which McCain regularly uses, perhaps more accurately than he intended, to designate anarchism).

Now McCain prowls all around this dilemma of anarchism, but he never really goes into it. Consequently he talks about anarchism as "a norm of social choice," when evidently it is not a usable norm—but rather is an alarm bell, or a lighthouse on a hidden reef. It serves not as a goal or ideal toward which we move, so much as a far-out warning against pushing egalitarianism too far—lest, like any other absolute, it destroy society absolutely.

Indeed, the individualistic model of choice offers a platform for the reactionary as well as the anarchist, for they can join together in saying of any society: "Love it—or leave it!" Instead of this cruel dilemma, this destructive "norm," surely the theory of public choice must concern itself with more humane and practical policies of pluralism and compromise, and feedbacks from experience.

It is significant that John Rawls, whose much-acclaimed *A Theory of Justice* has a strong anarchistic leaning, finds it advisable to allow for inequalities in the distribution of goods and services among persons. Rawls justifies this only if the inequalities conduce to improving the situation of the "least-advantaged" persons in the society. Now a critic may judge that, given the complexity of modern society, Rawls' doctrine could easily be used to justify any inequality, of whatever type and almost any degree—if only it would trickle down a little to the "lower classes," while simply disregarding any possibly better ways of attaining the same benefits. What we really need is not such "principles" embodying the naiveté of the egalitarian or the solipsism of the anarchist; we need informed economic and sociologic demonstrations that some inequalities may be socially tolerable even if technically unjust, and that other inequalities may be socially intolerable even if technically justified. It all depends not only on the net balance of benefits over costs in any proposal, but also on whether a specific kind and degree of inequality is or is not essential for social purposes of general current welfare or general secular development.

5

Trial of the Fact

GORDON TULLOCK*

The court, in most cases, faces decisions between two parties (one of which may be the state.) One of these two parties usually is interested in concealing or distorting the truth and/or misinterpreting the law. The other party (sometimes but not always) is interested in revealing the truth and interpreting the law correctly. This means that the court has a difficult problem in that there are people who are deliberately trying to deceive it. The problem would be difficult even without this complication. The court must do two things: first, it must determine what happened at some time in the past; and, second, it must determine the consequences of that happening in the past on the present situation, i.e., what is the legal consequence of these happenings in the past.

This paper is to be devoted to the first of these problems: the determination of the actual facts. The problem of the interpretation of the law or, in many cases, the interpretation of a contract which the law simply says shall be fulfilled, is left for another occasion. I shall not, however, discuss all aspects of the determination of the facts. Indeed, I am going to take a rather restricted approach. I will assume that there is some fixed technology, i.e., that the court procedures of necessity follow some specific routine, and simply discuss the amount of resources that should be invested in court pro-

---

* Professor of Economics, Virginia Polytechnic Institute and State University.

cedures, granted that the actual technology to be used has been predetermined.

Another subject that will be set aside is the desirability or undesirability of bias in the courts. It is a widely held belief that, at least in criminal proceedings, courts should be biased in favor of the accused, although Lenin thought that they should be biased in favor of the state. It is also widely believed that in civil procedures no such bias should exist.

Turning to problems of determining the facts, we should note that it is not an easy matter. Sometime in the past a body was discovered in an alley, with an ax wound in its head. It is now alleged that Mr. Smith was responsible for that ax wound. Mr. Smith, who presumably is the best-informed person on this matter, is motivated to lie if he was, indeed, responsible for the murder. If, on the other hand, he was not responsible for the murder, on the whole (and with certain special circumstances aside) he is motivated to tell the truth; but since we know that he has a great deal to gain from lying if he is guilty, we are apt to distrust his statements, even if he is innocent in the eye of God.

There may be very little in the way of other evidence; on the other hand, there may be quite a bit. In any event, however, the court is engaged in reconstructing an event in the past upon the evidence that has survived, and this evidence is surely a great deal less than complete. Further, there is surely someone who is arguing for the wrong, disarranging evidence, telling lies with the effort to confuse the court. There is a wrong side in this case, and the arguments presented for that side, the efforts used in generating information (or misinformation) for that side, and, as we have said before, the possible deliberate lying certainly make it harder for the court to reach a correct conclusion.

There seems to have been very little investigation of a formal nature aimed at determining the accuracy with which courts can reconstruct the past. Personally, and perhaps erroneously, I tend to conclude that the reason there has been so little investigation is simply that what little investigation has been done indicates that they are very inaccurate.

For example, it used to be (but no longer is) a custom for some professors in law schools to arrange that some exciting incident which had the appearance of a crime would occur before their class. They would then empanel a court and ask the individual students to act as witnesses before a jury (normally drawn from upper classmen of the law school) in order to determine what happened. The results tended to be very different indeed from what was known to have happened. This technique of teaching has been largely (but not wholly) abandoned, I think because it did bring the legal system into considerable disrepute with law students. Somewhat similar activities are sometimes undertaken in psychology courses, however, simply to demonstrate that people are poor observers. It is clear that a systematic approach to this type of experiment could give us a fair idea of how accurate the courts are. Once again, I suspect the reason it has not been done is because of fear as to the outcome of the experiment. It may be unpleasant to live in a society in which you are subject to a high probability of erroneous court decision, but it is perhaps pleasanter if you do not know how inaccurate it is.

Rather by accident, the jury project at the University of Chicago has produced some evidence on this point. They have had a number of different experiments in which essentially the same case is judged by different people. In some cases these are experimental juries empaneled for the experiment; in other cases they are the judge and the jury taken as separate entities in a real law case; and in one case in a third set of experiments, it is the true jury of a case and two experimental juries. In all cases, they show a good deal of difference among the outcomes. This clearly has to be put down to inaccuracy, although the particular method by which the project ran these experiments is such that you cannot tell how much of this inaccuracy is the result of misjudgment of fact and how much is the result of misjudgment of the legal consequences of the fact.

Last but not least, as evidence that the courts are not highly accurate, we have the fact that out-of-court settlements that are a compromise between the claims of the two parties are very common. Certainly at least 90 percent of all criminal actions, for example, are ended by what is called "negotiated plea," which is an out-of-court settlement. With respect to civil cases, we do not know the corresponding figure, but it is probably at least as high. The terms of these cases indicate that they discount risk. Such settlements can only occur when the skilled attorneys on both sides are uncertain as to the outcome of the judicial process. Clearly, if these attorneys, who, after all, are very well informed about the case (probably much better informed than either the judge or jury ever will be), are uncertain as to what the outcome should be, the outcome itself must have considerable inaccuracy.

Granted that there is some inherent risk of inaccuracy in the reconstruction of the facts as they occurred some time ago and that our court system presumably has a level of inaccuracy which is higher than inescapable minimum, it is sensible to discuss the characteristics of this inaccuracy and what we can call the optimal level. It will be recalled that we are using only one variable here, total resources. I doubt that anyone will object to our assumption that the level of accuracy can be increased by the investment of more resources and that this increase would be subject to declining marginal returns. A possible production function for accuracy is drawn as line P in Figure 1. Looked at from the standpoint of "society" and from that of *one* of the two parties (although we may not be sure which one), the indifference curves are of the nature shown as Line I, with 100 percent accuracy and zero resource investment (the upper left-hand corner) as the bliss point. The two lines are brought to a tangency in the usual way and, in Figure 1, we would choose to invest A resources in order to purchase A amount of accuracy.

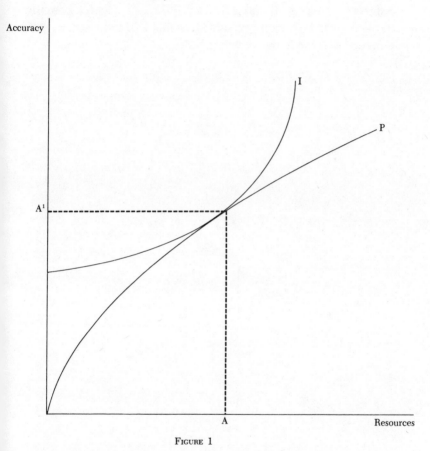

FIGURE 1

I have not specified where I got my indifference curve in Figure 1, but I hope the reader will permit me to defer discussion of this subject until later in this paper. That we, or at least someone, would be aiming at high accuracy at low cost (which is the general shape of these indifference curves) will, I trust, not seem very unlikely. We shall later discuss in greater detail the exact shape of such curves.

For the moment, however, let us return to the production functions which, as we shall see, are complicated enough. In Figure 2 we have production functions for two different cases, designated P and P'. P is a harder case in the sense that it requires more resource investment to get a given increment in accuracy.

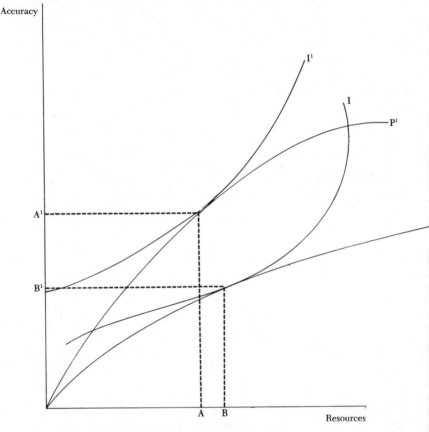

FIGURE 2

There is a simple operational way of measuring difficulty of a case. We could run exactly the same case, with the same resource investment, before a collection of different decision-makers, and then determine how many of them went right and how many went wrong. The University of Chicago jury project, using film, had more or less done this with respect to two cases and, from examining the results of the two cases, it is clear that in one of the two there was much more error than in the other. It is, of course, not essential that we even know what the correct decision is, since the case in which we had the greater diversity of opinion among the decision-making groups or individuals would be the one that we would list as "harder," unless we are taking a very uncharitable view of the accuracy of our decision-making procedure.

With these two production functions for accuracy, then, we fit the same family of indifference curves as in Figure 1 and we observe that, with the easier of the two cases, we invest A amount of resources and get A′ accuracy; with the more difficult case, we invest more resources and would get less accuracy, as shown by B, B′. It is obvious from inspection that it would be quite possible for us to choose to invest less resources in the harder case than in the easier case, and get even less accuracy, if our indifference curves were shaped just a little bit differently. This is not at all improbable in some cases. Different cases, of course, have different degrees of difficulty. In Figure 3 we have arranged the cases along the horizontal axis so that the easiest ones are at the left and the most difficult at the right.

Note that there has been a change in the accuracy level shown in Figures 1, 2, and 3. In Figure 2, the origin essentially is the accuracy of flipping a coin, i.e., 0.5. In Figure 3, it is possible to get accuracy less than 0.5. If, however, we had the kind of information which is necessary to draw up the set of curves for Figure 2 for each and every case before it began, we would never get less than 0.5 accuracy. At the point where line A in Figure 3—which shows the accuracy to be obtained by this optimal method—reaches the 0.5 line, we would switch to flipping a coin, and hence

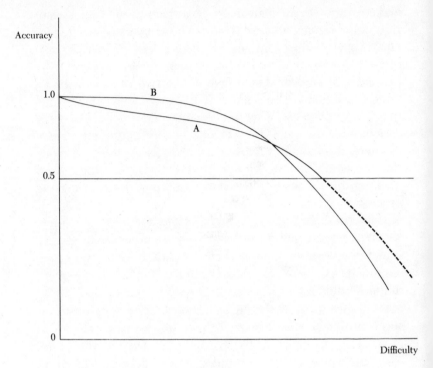

FIGURE 3

would stay at 0.5. If we did not make this switch, then the dotted line which extends line A below the 0.5 line would be the result. Assuming, however, that we have this perfect knowledge of the difficulty of the case which has been displayed in Figures 1 and 2, we would not use the dotted part of the line.

In the real world, of course, we do not have this perfect knowledge. Let us assume, for example, that we simply have a general idea of the level of difficulty of some category of cases but cannot distinguish among them. In fact, some are more difficult than others but we do not know in advance which is which. Under these circumstances, we would have to select some degree of resource commitment which would be given to the average case. If some outside source then arranged the cases along the difficulty axis as in Figure 3 and told us the resulting accuracy level, it would look somewhat like line B. Note that in this case the line does indeed go below 0.5 because there are some cases in which the evidence is positively misleading. In general, with a constant resource investment for all cases, we receive more accuracy than we would like in the easier cases and less in the more difficult cases.

In the real world, of course, it is possible to make some guesses as to how difficult cases are; hence, the resource commitment to the cases can be varied to some extent according to their difficulty. It is unlikely that the perfect adjustment of line A could be achieved, however. What would actually occur is some line between A and B with relative overinvestment of resources for the easier cases and relative underinvestment for the harder cases. It is particularly unfortunate that we cannot detect those cases in which the evidence is positively misleading, because in those cases we are apt to spend a good deal of resources in achieving an erroneous result. The cheap method of flipping a coin would clearly be an impovement, if we could only tell in which cases it is better.

Note that when we say we cannot tell which are the most difficult cases, this is in part because the "we" referred to is not the parties. Presumably the parties in most (although not all) cases know what the correct outcome is and have some idea of the probability of the court reaching that outcome. Thus, if we were to the right of the point in Figure 3 where the line showing accuracy crosses the 0.5 level, the two parties might be well aware of this fact. The judge would not, and of course one of the parties would deny very vigorously in court that this was so. For example, suppose that some kind of transaction has taken place between a man who was a vigorous and convincing liar and a man who had certain mannerisms that made it appear to most people that he was lying even when he was telling the

ECONOMICS OF PUBLIC CHOICE

truth. The professional liar had cheated the truthful man, who would make a very poor witness. Presumably it would be clear to both of these parties that A, the liar, had lied and the other party was telling the truth, and that the court was likely to reach the opposite conclusion. Thus, the case would appear to be beyond the point where the accuracy level crosses the 0.5 level to them and in the eye of God, but the court might think of it as a rather simple open-and-shut case in which an obvious liar (the man who had not lied) was attempting to cheat a sincere and truthful man (the liar). Under these circumstances, the court might place a case which actually lay near the right-hand end of our diagram at the left.

With a finite chance of error being attached to *all* legal cases, the individual contemplating breaking the law or perhaps violating a contract always has at least some chance of getting away with it. We deal with this by seeing to it that the present discounted value of the breach is, at least in most cases, negative because whatever happens to him— i.e., court costs plus whatever penalty is assessed—is greater than the probable gain from the inaccuracy of the court. Unfortunately, this subject cannot be discussed in detail without a discussion of bias in the court proceedings; and cannot be dealt with in full without discussion of out-of-court settlements. Both of these subjects must be deferred until another occasion.

For the moment, I have to make a rather limited assumption on the subject. This assumption is that the individuals will not, in fact, violate the law or break a contract unless they have a reasonably good chance of getting away with it. In other words, the cost if the violation is highly likely to be detected by the court would be greater than the benefits, but if there is a fairly good chance of getting away with it, then breach is sensible. With this very simple assumption, we observe a rather paradoxical characteristic of accuracy in court proceedings.

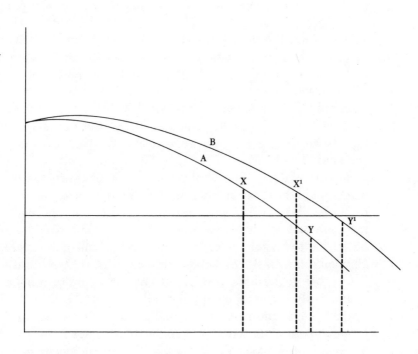

FIGURE 4

In Figure 4, we show accuracy and difficulty of cases in the usual way and with two different resource investments, A and B. B is a higher level of resource investment, and hence leads to a higher degree of accuracy than does A. Once we have made the assumption that the individual will not break the law or breach the contract unless he has a fair chance of getting away with it, then unless the probability of error is fairly sizeable, he will keep the contract or obey the law. For simplicity, assume that he will be willing to breach the contract or violate the law when the difficulty of the case is to the right of X and not do so when it is to the left of X with accuracy level A. The other party will choose to bring action at law against the breachor of the contract or the violator of the law only if he has at least a reasonable prospect of winning; hence, he will only bring litigation if the case falls to the left of Y. Thus, with accuracy level A we would have the cases from the origin to X in which no violation of the law or contract occurs. The distance from point X to the right boundary of our diagram would indicate those cases in which it would be profitable to breach the contract or violate the law. But the cases which are actually brought before the court would only be those which lie between X and Y. Over this range, the court would have about a 50-50 accuracy rate.

Suppose we move now to a more accurate court, the one represented by line B, and with a higher investment of resources. With this higher level of accuracy in the court, the potential law violator or contract breachor would not be willing to breach under the same circumstances as before. He would now insist that the case be at least X' level of difficulty before he breached. Similarly, his opposite number would only be willing to actually undertake litigation against him if the case lay to the left of Y'. Cases actually brought before the court would be those between X' and Y', and would have about the same level of accuracy as those brought to the less accurate court.

The paradox is clear. Improving the accuracy of the court in some potential sense, which is all we can hope to do, does not improve the accuracy of the court over the particular cases brought before it. The cases brought before it are brought by parties who have taken the accuracy into account and are only willing to bring them into court if they have a reasonable chance of winning, granted the amount of accuracy. Thus, improving the accuracy of the court does not mean that it decides the cases before it in a more accurate manner; it changes the cases before it. The gain from improving the accuracy of the court from A to B in Figure 4 is the fact that, in cases where the degree of difficulty lies between X and X', the law is carried out with level of accuracy B and not carried out with level of accuracy A. We do not contest that this is a desirable goal, but it is odd that it takes this form rather than improvement in the accuracy of the court. It also, of course, makes it somewhat difficult to measure the accuracy of the court by examining cases which actually come before it.

In selecting a degree of accuracy, in essence we are partitioning the cases into those in which there will be perfect enforcement because the party contemplating violating the law decides not to because the odds are too heavily against him; into those in which there will be reasonably even odds and frequent breaches; and into those in which the party who breaches the law in fact will get away with it. An increase in the accuracy of the court improves the size of the first category and reduces the size of the second and third categories. If there are resources invested in court proceedings, then the reduction of the total number of court cases brought as accuracy improves may mean that there is no great increase in the total amount of resource invested, as the resource commitment to each individual case is increased.

Equation (1) shows the cost of some individual case:

$$(1) \qquad C = R + f(R)E$$

C, representing cost, is on the left; and R, resources, is to the right. The resources invested in the case are, of course, direct costs of that case. I have been assuming, however, that the accuracy of the case outcome is a function of the resources, shown by $f(R)$. In this case, it is an inverse function, i.e., I am measuring the inaccuracy rather than the accuracy; so as R goes up, $f(R)$ goes down. Lastly, there is some cost associated with an erroneous outcome, and that is shown by E. Thus the cost of the litigation taken as a whole is the investment in resources in it, together with the probability that it will go wrong and the cost of that error.

The accuracy of the court, which in our present model

is a function of the resources invested, is more prominently displayed in changing the cases that are brought before it than in changing outcomes. Thus, as the accuracy of the court increases, the probability that a given case will be brought goes down and the total number of cases goes down. This is shown in equation (2):

$$(2) \qquad C = g(R) [R + f(R) \cdot E] - h(R)$$

The function of R which relates the investment of resources to the number of breaches which occur is denoted by $g(R)$. As R increases, the value of the function should go down, since fewer cases where breach is profitable will appear. The cost of the litigation itself from equation (1) is then multiplied by this function. We still have one final correction, however. In those cases in which evidence is so misleading, granted the degree of accuracy of the court, that the other party will not bother to bring the action, we still have the cost of error, i.e., the outcome is wrong. However, we do save the resources that otherwise would be invested in the court. This is shown by another function of R, $h(R)$, at the end of equation (2).

This equation has the rather surprising characteristic that it is possible (albeit unlikely) that increasing R will actually reduce C over the entire range. In other words, we should put infinite resources into every single legal case, because, if we are willing to invest infinite resources, no legal cases will arise.

This apparently paradoxical outcome is, of course, only a possibility. Probably the shape of the g, f, and h functions is such that the return on resources invested in litigation is, even in terms of equation (2), marginally declining, and hence there is an optimal amount of resource investment. This is particularly likely since it is probable that merely maintaining a judicial system in existence of necessity imposes at least some costs, and these minimum costs must be divided across the number of cases that occur. If the number of cases is pushed down to a low enough level, the costs of the apparatus might be quite high, even if there were very few cases. But, in this area what we need is further research in order to get some idea of the shape of these functions.

So much for the cost function. Our figures have also shown indifference curves. These indifference curves can be assumed to be individual indifference curves, on the assumption that individuals have something to gain from correctly carrying out the law. As a second possibility, they could be the indifference curves of the two parties to a contract at the time the contract is drawn up. Or, thirdly, they could be some kind of social indifference curves. If they are the latter, they would be the product of a specified process for aggregating individual preferences. In a democracy these decisions are made largely by legislatures elected by the people and various court officials, in particular district attorneys who, in most parts of the United States (although not all), are also elected. If we wish to be romantic, we can say that this represents in some sense the popular will. More accurately, it represents the outcome of a process which has been so designed that it is, at least to some extent, influenced by popular views. Whether we should call these curves indifference curves and refer to preference functions is, I think, a little dubious, but we can refer to them as behavior curves generated by a special set of institutions. Since I have devoted a great deal of my professional life to discussing the type of institutions involved in democracy, I would like to skip the subject here and merely refer the reader to my other writings.

We have now completed our discussion of the problem of accuracy in the trial of the facts. The reader may have found the discussion tedious and boring, but so far as I know these issues have never before been discussed with any degree of rigor. It is not obvious that our fairly rigorous model will provide any better decision-making procedure than the rather vague ideas that now float around in the literature. Nevertheless, it does at least point the direction for further empirical research and indicates what we could do if we did have better empirical knowledge. It seems to me that one (albeit only one) of the reasons that there has been so little empirical research in problems of judicial accuracy has been the absence of any formal models into which the results of such research could be incorporated. Indeed, if you read the general literature, the question of whether there is even an implicit and vague model immediately comes to mind.

Comments on
"Trial of the Fact"

Alvin L. Marty[*]

Let me preface my remarks before this jury by stating that I am innocent of the charge of having competent knowledge in the area of law and economics. As a monetary theorist, I am commenting on Prof. Tullock's intriguing paper from one viewpoint: does the economic theory make sense?

Tullock's paper deals with both positive and normative economics. On the one hand, what is the optimal amount of resources that society should invest in court procedures in order to determine accuracy? On the other hand, what model is the appropriate one in order to test empirically what actually happens? Tullock assumes a production function relating resource flow input to the output of accuracy and gives it the usual shape of the total productive curve, relating, for example, increments of output to increments of capital per unit labor. But what, in this case, is the fixed factor which is causing diminishing returns so that the marginal product of resources in producing accuracy falls? Why not constant returns to scale: doubling the resources doubles accuracy, so that a finite amount of resources is needed to produce 100 per cent accuracy. Is the curve like a Cobb-Douglas in which an increase of the resource flow per unit (what?) leads to an increase in accuracy which approaches but never reaches an upper asymptote? I frankly

[*] Professor of Economics, The City College of the City University of New York.

don't know but I plead guilty to having been made queasy by Tullock's construction.

Next Tullock appends "societal" indifference curves between accuracy, which is a "good," and the resource flow, which is a "bad," so that indifference curves which are higher and to the left represent levels of utility. Along an indifference curve society becomes less willing to trade an increment in resource cost for a given increment in accuracy as the resource input increases. Optimality is reached when the marginal rate of substitution between accuracy and resource input is equal to the marginal rate of transformation of resources into accuracy. But what determines the shape of these indifference curves? Why, as Tullock states, should the indifference curves become straight lines in the case of risk neutrality and slightly concave upwards if the "parties" are risk averse? Here Tullock loses me completely. Risk aversion and neutrality are concepts which only have meaning under uncertainty. But under uncertainty (which in this case is at the heart of the problem), the sharp dichotomy between tastes and opportunities which allows us to use indifference curves is shattered.

Let us turn now to what is perhaps the most intriguing observation in the paper. Tullock notes that since court cases differ in difficulty, we don't want to make an overall average resource commitment but rather plow the difficult cases more intensively. (Of course, judgment as to which cases are most difficult can be at times erroneous.) This leads to a paradox: when you increase the accuracy of the court, you eliminate some potential cases so that fewer of the less difficult cases are brought before the court and the degree of accuracy achieved *ex post* may in fact remain unchanged. To formalize this paradox Tullock introduces two equations: (1) $C = R + f(R) E$, where C is the total cost of *an individual* case and is equal to the sum of resources devoted to obtaining accuracy plus the cost of an inaccurate output (E) weighted by the probability of an inaccurate outcome. This probability itself is a function $f(R)$ of the resource input.

What is the total cost of all cases brought before all courts? To answer this Tullock introduces the following equation:

$$C^+ = g(R) \cdot [R + f(R)E] - h(R).$$

When evidence is so misleading that the other party doesn't bother to bring action, then $h(R)$ is the resources the court saves even though the outcome is wrong. I am not sure I understand the role of $h(\text{R})$. Does an increase in accuracy leads to a rise in $h(R)$? My own preference would be to eliminate $h(R)$ entirely. C^+ on the left-hand side now represents the cost of all cases (it doesn't help matters that Tullock uses the same C in both equations) where the number of cases itself is a function of $R - g(R)$. Tullock speculates, somewhat jocularly, that it may be the case that as R approaches infinity, $g(R)$ approaches zero. This is the Tullock paradox in its purest form.

Let me end by gently chiding Tullock for his claim to having provided a fairly rigorous model. Perhaps an improvement over previous work, provocative and intriguing, yes; but rigorous, no. However, this is a minor fault in a paper which, like all good papers, raises more questions than it answers.

6

Towards a Consumption Theory of Political Democracy

MORRIS SILVER[*]

The creation and perpetuation of states is accomplished by coercion (conquest) or consent (general will or social contract). Clearly, a study of the possible economic forces helping to determine historical trends in the relative importance of coercion and consent is needed. The present paper focuses upon a somewhat narrower question: the emergence of systems of *active* consent.

The active element is not altogether absent even in the most authoritarian states. For example:

Chingas Khan proceeded through two stages in the establishment of his power. In the first he gathered his personal following. . . . In the second he sent messages to all the nomads and assembled them to witness, participate in, and support his election as Mongol Khan. By their assembly they expressed their consent. [25, p. 102]

Similarly, according to Herodotus, the Medes who had assembled to discuss their severe crime problem agreed to introduce a system of monarchy with a respected citizen (Deioces) as king [29, pp. 66-67]. Obviously, however, the active element is much more pronounced in modern democ-

---

[*] Professor of Economics, The City College of the City University of New York. I wish to thank R. D. Auster, Gary S. Becker, Benjamin Klebaner, Alvin Marty, George Schwab, and G. Sirkin for their helpful comments on an earlier version of this paper.

racies[1] which universally distribute the franchise and elect the rulers periodically and freely.

Increases in the size of social groups have long been recognized to work against political democracy, but more recently it has been suggested that autocratic systems in the presence of economic development tend to give way to more democratic systems. The objective in what follows is to expand on the hints in the literature and discuss in a more systematic way the possible role of *income* in the making of decisions concerning what can be termed the "democrativeness" of political systems.

I. EVIDENCE

The existence of a positive (but by no means perfect) relationship between income levels and "democrativeness" of political systems is supported by different types of evidence. Casual observation suggests that today's most affluent nations typically have more democratically selected states. Moreover, the emergence or extension of political democracy in widely different times and places is clearly linked to increases in income.

In England the political pressure of the 1820's and 30's, culminating in the enfranchisement of the new middle class by the Reform Act of 1832 [5, 46, 49], was accompanied by a sharp rise in the real income of this social stratum [10]. Similarly, increases in the real wages of industrial and agricultural workers in the latter half of the nineteenth century [10] coincided with, amid renewed political pressure and popular violence, the enfranchisement of male workers by the statutes of 1867 and 1884 [43, 46, 49].

The Japanese "Taishō Democracy" movement (1912–1924) enfranchised the bulk of the middle classes by 1919 and culminated in 1925 in the passage of a universal manhood suffrage bill. In the early stages the demand for democratic reforms came primarily from businessmen [35], who were enjoying unprecedented profits during the war boom of 1914–19 [30, p. 39]. Real industrial wages were apparently stationary during the war, but during 1920–24 there was a precipitous rise in both real wages [30, p. 144] and demands by lower-economic-status urban dwellers to be allowed to participate in politics [35].

The New Zealand Act of 1879 which significantly extended the suffrage as compared to the Reform Act of 1832 [27, pp. 19–26] was immediately preceded by strong economic growth stimulated by gold rushes (1860-69) and an investment boom (1870–78) [8, pp. 31–37].

In Argentina rapidly rising incomes (during the 1880's and especially during 1904–1912) and a prolonged political struggle immediately preceded the passage of the 1912 law calling for universal male suffrage by secret ballot and the democratic election of 1916 [17; 39, pp. 196–204].

With the suffrage reforms of 1907–1909 and 1918–1921, Sweden became a true parliamentary democracy [2, pp. 30–31]. The 1890's period, in which the suffrage movement gathered increasing force [2, p. 31], was also a period of generally rising living standards due to a significant upsurge in industrial development [38, pp. 187, 199, 210–11].

Danish democracy, which drew its mass support from the peasantry, grew with reforms in 1834 and 1848 and finally triumphed in the 1880's. The peasants' demand for democratization of the political order (e.g., via the Farmer's Leagues in the 1840's and the United Left party of the 1870's) has been traced to a prior increase in their wealth resulting from the decision of the Reventlow Commission (1784) to give the peasants land and credit [31, pp. 255–56; 33, pp. 30–36].

In Athens the reforms of Solon (594 B.C.), which freed those enslaved for debt, wiped out the debts of farmers, and removed the mortgages from their properties, taken together with growing general affluence from changes in agriculture and trade [19, pp. 164–68], inaugurated the drive toward democratic rule [28, pp. 78–79]. Later, in 508, when the popular council was dissolved, the angry disfranchised masses successfully revolted and recalled Cleisthenes (the "second founder of Athenian democracy") [50, pp. 140–41].

The early history of Rome is obscure, but apparently the land distribution of 393 B.C., whereby all citizens secured a share of captured (Veian) land immediately north of the city, significantly improved the economic status of the "proletariat" [13, pp. 48–50]. In 366 B.C., after an intense "patrician versus plebian" struggle, the consulship (the highest magistracy in the state) was opened to plebeians [4, p. 55]. A period of land distributions of newly conquered territories also preceded a "secession of the plebs" and the passage of a law in 287 B.C. establishing equal manhood suffrage in legislation for the "plebeians" [13, pp. 49–50; 4, pp. 57–58].

After 1347–1350 in Western Europe, wage rates rose sharply while land values declined as a consequence of the Black Death which reduced the population by a third or more [20, pp. 32–35]. In the following decades (the "golden age of wage labor") many cities experienced democratic agitation on the part of artisans and laborers who sought the rights of citizenship (the franchise to use modern terms) via full membership in a guild. The clearest example is provided by the revolt of the Florentine wool-workers in 1378 (the revolt of the *Ciompi*) who henceforth were to appoint three of the nine city magistrates [20, p. 119; 3, pp. 149–50, 380]. Other worker rebellions occurred in Lyons, Paris, and Cologne [45, p. 403]. It seems quite possible that similar causes contributed to the demand for an end to villeinage and the related social stigma [22, pp. 209–11] in the English Peasants Revolt of 1381 and to the numerous local peasant revolts in other parts of Western Europe after the middle of the fourteenth century [12, pp. 137–39, 266–67].

The cases of Argentina and Japan are particularly instructive because in both countries democratic rule was apparently aborted by the depression of the 1930's. Again, Cobban [6, p. 255] has noted that the era of dictatorships beginning at the time of the Gracchi (133–123 B.C.) coincides rather neatly with the exhaustion of free land in Italy and the end of the great age of Roman frontier expansion.

Wolf [48] finds a positive and statistically significant simple correlation between an index of political democracy and real per capita gross national product in a group of Latin American countries. Adelman and Morris consider a group of less developed countries and conclude that "the coefficients resulting from the factor analysis indicate that a typically western configuration of political traits is generally associated with higher average income" [1, p. 566].

Lipset [26] classifies European and English-speaking countries as "stable democracies" or as "unstable democracies" and finds that average income is higher in the former than in the latter group of countries. He also observes that average income is higher in those Latin American countries classified as "democracies and unstable dictatorships."

In a study of forty-seven developing countries Simpson [41] observes a positive correlation between a measure of political participation and national income. Cutright [9] constructs an index of political development (understood in a democratic sense) covering the period 1940–1960 for seventy-seven nations. He finds this index to be positively correlated with an index of economic development. Hagen [18] classifies the political structures of underdeveloped countries as "authoritarian," "semicompetitive," and "competitive" and observes that a composite index of economic development tends to increase as one moves from the former to the latter classification.

Smith [42] observes positive and often statistically significant correlation and regression coefficients between a refined version of Cutright's "index of democrativeness" and indices of urbanization, education, and communications development. His regressions are for the period 1946–1965 and explain behavior in 100 nations or in various geographic sub-samples of these nations.

II. INTERPRETATIONS

When we move to the interpretation of the positive relationship, unanimity is replaced by great diversity. A few examples should be sufficient to give the flavor of the discussion.

Some students argue that poverty-stricken populations tend to become desperate and seek quick authoritarian solutions [48, p. 2]. According to Lipson:

Where more people own at least some property, they have something to conserve and are therefore less disposed to extremist attitudes and violent actions—both of which militate against democracy. Psychologically, where the basic needs of food, clothing, and shelter are satisfied with a reasonable amount of comfort, the resulting sense of security promotes a tendency to compromise and moderation. [28, pp. 245–46]

Lipset argues that:

Increased wealth is not only related causally to the development of democracy by changing the social conditions of the workers, but it also affects the political role of the middle class through changing the shape of the stratification structure so that it shifts from an elongated pyramid, with a large lower class base, to a diamond with a growing middle class. A large middle class plays a mitigating role in moderating conflict since it is able to reward moderate and democratic parties and penalize extremist groups. [26, p. 83]

while Hagen believes the

expansion of industrial activity, even if it is a gradual growth of small enterprises rather than a spectacular change, creates a middle class with interests opposed to those of a traditional ruling landed group. Increased industrialization, urbanization, and geographic movement widen horizons and create new ambitions. All of these changes breed political change. [18, p. 10]

Adelman and Morris do not believe that economic development and political democracy are causally related. To them it appears more plausible to . . . ascribe the positive association . . . to the existence of common forces which underlie the transformations of social institutions which typically accompany economic development and the changes in political structure characteristic of the evolution of modern political systems. [1, p. 566]

The positive relationship between income and democracy has been interpreted in political, psychological, and sociological terms. Surprisingly, economic interpretations have been both rare and ambiguous.

The line of explanation followed here is, first, that the democratic process in which consent is actively (or expressly) given is itself a consumer good, and, second, that in mass societies democratic systems are generally more expensive to operate than autocratic systems.[2]

The first possibility receives some support from White and Lippitt:

Of all the generalizations growing out of the experimental study of groups, one of the most broadly and firmly established is that the members of a group tend to be more satisfied if they have at least some feeling of participation in its decisions. . . . *If democracy is really democracy and not laissez-faire*—i.e., if it emphasizes strong leadership and other factors that make for efficiency—*it is usually more satisfying than autocracy*. This is true at least in our own culture and probably also in most other cultures of the world. [47, pp. 260–69]

Another piece of evidence supporting the view that individuals derive satisfaction from the act of participation in political decision-making is provided by the extent to which they actually do participate within democratic mass societies. Political activity is not without cost to the individual. In mass societies, and in the absence of coercion, it is quite rational for the individual to abstain from political activity on the grounds that the nature and quality of political decisions are independent of his own political activities and that, as a citizen, he will receive whatever benefits flow from political decisions even if he does not participate in making them.[3]

Measures facilitating mass participation in state-making tend to be quite costly. Aside from the money costs of framing a constitution, establishing political parties, holding meetings and elections, protecting minority rights, and gathering and assimilating various kinds of information, including the "disclosure or notice of prospective actions and the announcement of the considerations underlying actions" [24, p. 17], there are the imputed costs of the participants' time. Carl Cohen concludes that in larger communities "the physical machinery of participation becomes exceedingly complicated and very expensive" [7, p. 108]. The effect of increases in population and territory ruled is illustrated by the demise of "direct" democracy in city-states of Early Dynastic Sumer [19, pp. 37–45], republics of Vedic India [44, p. 51], Rome [4, pp. 8–9; 29, pp. 246–77], and of "town meetings" the world over.

It seems, on the whole, probable that the mass communication system accompanying modern economic development operates to reduce the relative cost of both modern (or representative or indirect) and direct democracy.[4] The cases of Japan in the 1930's and of China today suggest that development also reduces the relative cost of the totalitarian variant of autocracy. Nevertheless, it is clear that once societies have exceeded some minimum size the cost of state-making is lower under autocratic systems such as kingship for life, hereditary (next-of-kin or rotating) kingship, adoptive kingship, aristocracy, divination, or *coup d'etat*, which helps to account for their historical popularity[5]

The remainder of the argument is best understood by means of a simple analogy. When an individual's income is low, he might deem it unwise to use part of it to purchase butter or a Cadillac. In order to be better able to satisfy more urgent needs, he might instead purchase margarine or a Duster, or perhaps do without a table spread or a car. However, at higher levels of income consumers might feel they could afford these items and purchase them. If the assumptions presented above are accepted, a similar argument can be made for active consent in mass societies. At low levels of income, people might prefer to do without democracy (they would not revolt or otherwise bear the cost of resisting authoritarian rule) in order to satisfy more pressing needs, but as development proceeds and incomes rise they might feel better able to afford it and increasingly engage in or support political activity designed to achieve a democratic system or to maintain democratic rights.[6,7]

III.   CONCLUDING OBSERVATIONS

Section I summarized a growing body of evidence suggesting that income and democrativeness of political systems are positively correlated. A representative sample of the current interpretations of this relationship was presented in Section II. Section II then suggested that the desire for democracy, like that for caviar and Cadillacs, is limited by its relative cost and responds positively to changes in the level of per capita income. However, the stress placed upon income should not be taken to mean that other economic and non-economic variables are not relevant or are less important. A more complex theory might explain not only the general tendency noted above, but a number of "deviant" cases.

A major weakness of existing quantitative studies is that single-equation estimates of the coefficient of income must be suspect when there is a reasonable likelihood that political democracy is a determinant of national income. Of course, econometricians have provided us with several simultaneous-equation techniques and, in principle, one of these could be employed to provide an unbiased estimate of the impact of income on the demand for political democracy. It would be more difficult to empirically disentangle my argument from the view that countries differ in their distributions of various personal characteristics (i.e., in their "national characters") and that certain of these (e.g., a spirit of enterprise and industry, an inquisitive mind, or good health) are responsible for both higher incomes and heightened desires to participate in state-making.

NOTES

1. Lipset defines modern or "liberal" democracy as a "political system which supplies regular constitutional opportunities for changing the governing officials. It is a social mechanism for the resolution of the problem of societal decision making among conflicting interest groups which permits the largest part of the population to influence the decisions through their ability to choose among alternative contenders for political office. In large measure . . . this definition implies a number of specific conditions: (a) a 'political formula,' a system of beliefs, legitimizing the democratic system and specifying the institutions—parties, a free press, and so forth—which are legitimized, i.e., accepted as proper by all; (b) one set of political leaders in office; and (c) one or more sets of leaders, out of office, who act as a legitimate opposition attempting to gain office" [26, p. 71]. Or as MacIver puts it: "Democracy is not a way of governing . . . but primarily a way of determining who shall govern and, broadly, to what ends. . . . The people . . . do not and cannot govern; they control the government" [32, p. 59]. Mayo agrees and adds that "political systems can be classified as more or less democratic according to a number of criteria [periodic mass elections, equal voting, political freedoms] associated with popular control and designed to make it effective; only if a particular system meets the tests of a substantial number of these criteria do we . . . call it democratic" [32, p. 60].

2. Although the arguments are quite different, I sympathize with the conclusions reached by David M. Potter. According to this historian "the principles of democracy are not universal truths, ignored during centuries of intellectual darkness . . . but rather . . . democracy is the foremost by far of the many advantages which our economic affluence has brought us" [34, pp. 117–18]. Alvin Marty recently called my attention to a similar statement of J. R. Hicks that increases in wealth facilitate the demand for "liberal democratic goods."

3. For a more complete discussion and references to the literature see [40]. Most studies report a positive correlation between the income of individuals and their political participation (see the useful exchange in *Public Choice* [14, 15, 16, 37]).

4. It seems doubtful that among historical states active consent ever took the form of "direct" democracy without any meaningful

trace of "representation." Even in ancient Athens the ten elected "generals" and the elected Council of 500 may have represented the citizens. "The Council carried on all negotiations with foreign states and received ambassadors; it directed foreign policy. In internal affairs, too, almost everything was under its care; the officials had to report to it; it had supreme authority over all financial matters. Finally, its judicial functions had not entirely gone . . . [and] the Council had a certain right of punishment, especially over officials" [11, p. 64]. Moreover, since the Council (or its committee) prepared and guided the affairs of the popular assembly, it was certainly able to make important negative decisions [21, pp. 28, 46]. A more fundamental question is raised by the absence of women in the Athenian popular assembly. Did this absence reflect a strong and sexually shared view of the appropriate sexual division of labor? Is it conceivable that even in the absence of formal elections the adult males were generally regarded as the representatives of their mothers, sisters, and wives?

5. The anthropologist Hoebel observes that hereditary monarchy "is so common among advanced primitive societies that we must conclude that the need for centralized control outweighs the urge for democratic freedom at this level of social development. The resurgence of democracy comes later" [23, p. 527].

6. In the event that democratic selection of the state results in a more nearly optimal provision of state services and/or reduces the exploitative component of the rulers' incomes, the argument in the text requires that these benefits to the population would be more than offset by the additional cost of establishing and maintaining democracy.

7. In the perspective of the present paper, H. B. Mayo's assertion that democracy in Athens did not depend on slavery but that the "financial returns [only] enabled Athens to live at a higher standard, and to erect the Parthenon and other magnificent public buildings" [32, p. 43] is of dubious validity.

REFERENCES

1. Adelman, Irma and Cynthia Taft Morris. "Factor Analysis of the Interrelationship Between Social and Political Variables and Per Capita GNP," *Quarterly Journal of Economics* (November, 1965), pp. 555–78.

2. Board, Joseph B., Jr. *The Government and Politics of Sweden* (Boston: Houghton Mifflin Co., 1970).

3. Brucker, Gene A. *Florentine Politics and Society: 1343–1378* (Princeton, New Jersey: Princeton University Press, 1962).

4. Brunt, P. A. *Social Conflicts in the Roman Republic* (New York: W. W. Norton and Co., 1971).

5. Cahill, Gilbert A. *The Great Reform Bill of 1832* (Lexington, Mass.: D. C. Heath and Co., 1969).
6. Cobban, Alfred. *Dictatorship* (New York: Charles Scribner's & Sons, 1939).
7. Cohen, Carl. *Democracy* (Athens, Georgia: University of Georgia Press, 1971).
8. Condliffe, J. B. *New Zealand in the Making*, 2nd. ed. (London: Allen and Unwin, Ltd., 1959).
9. Cutright, Phillips. "National Political Development," *American Sociological Review* (April, 1963), pp. 253–64.
10. Deane, Phyllis. *The First Industrial Revolution* (Cambridge, England: Cambridge University Press, 1965).
11. Ehrenberg, Victor. *The Greek State*, 2nd. ed. (London: Methuen & Co., Ltd., 1969).
12. Ferguson, Wallace K. *Europe in Transition: 1300–1520* (Boston: Houghton Mifflin Co., 1962).
13. Frank, Tenney. *An Economic History of Rome*, 2nd. ed. (Baltimore: Johns Hopkins Press, 1927).
14. Fraser, John. "Comment," *Public Choice* (Fall, 1972), pp. 115–18.
15. Frey, Bruno S. "Why Do High Income People Participate More in Politics?" *Public Choice* (Fall, 1971), pp. 101–105.
16. –––––. "Reply," *Public Choice* (Fall, 1972), pp. 119–22.
17. Germani, G. "The Transition to a Mass Democracy in Argentina," in S. N. Eisenstadt, ed., *Readings in Social Evolution and Development* (London: Pergamon Press, 1970), pp. 313–36.
18. Hagen, Everett E. "A Framework for Analyzing Economic and Political Change," in *Development of the Emerging Countries: An Agenda for Research* (Washington, D. C.: The Brookings Institute, 1962), pp. 1–38.
19. Hammond, Mason. *The City in the Ancient World* (Cambridge, Mass.: Harvard University Press, 1972).
20. Hay, Denys. *Europe in the Fourteenth and Fifteenth Centuries* (New York: Holt, Rinehart, and Winston, Inc., 1966).
21. Hermens, Frederick A. *The Representative Republic* (Notre Dame, Indiana: University of Notre Dame Press, 1958).
22. Hodgett, Gerald A. J. *A Social and Economic History of Medieval Europe* (London: Methuen & Co.., Ltd., 1972).
23. Hoebel, E. Adamson. *Anthropology: The Study of Man*, 4th ed. (New York: McGraw-Hill, 1972).
24. Key, V. O., Jr. *Public Opinion and American Democracy* (New York: Alfred A. Knopf, 1964).
25. Krader, Lawrence. *Formation of the State* (New York: Prentice-Hall, 1968).
26. Lipset, Seymour M. "Some Social Requisites of Democracy: Economic Development and Political Legitimacy," *American Political Science Review* (March, 1959), pp. 65–105.

27. Lipson, Leslie. *The Politics of Equality* (Chicago: University of Chicago Press, 1948).

28. —————. *The Democratic Civilization* (New York: Oxford University Press, 1964).

29. —————. *The Great Issues of Politics,* 4th. ed. (Englewood Cliffs, N. J.: Prentice-Hall, Inc., 1970).

30. Lockwood, William C. *The Economic Development of Japan* (Princeton, New Jersey: Princeton University Press, 1954).

31. McCord, William. *The Springtime of Freedom* (New York: Oxford University Press, 1965).

32. Mayo, H. B. *An Introduction to Democratic Theory* (New York: Oxford University Press, 1960).

33. Miller, Kenneth E. *Government and Politics in Denmark* (Boston: Houghton Mifflin Co., 1968).

34. Potter, David M. *People of Plenty: Economic Abundance and the American Character* (Chicago: University of Chicago Press, 1964).

35. Reischauer, Edwin O. *Japan: Past and Present* (New York: Alfred A. Knopf, Inc., 1964).

36. Rostow, W. W. *Politics and the Stages of Growth* (Cambridge, Mass.: Cambridge University Press, 1971).

37. Russell, Keith P. "Comment," *Public Choice* (Fall, 1972), pp. 113–14.

38. Samuelson, Kurt. *From Great Power to Welfare State* (London: Allen and Unwin, Ltd., 1968).

39. Scobie, James R. *Argentina: A City and a Nation,* 2nd. ed. (New York: Oxford University Press, 1971).

40. Silver, Morris. "A Demand Analysis of Voting Costs and Voting Participation," *Social Science Research,* Vol. 2, No. 2 (August, 1973), pp. 111–24.

41. Simpson, R. "The Congruence of the Political, Social, and Economic Aspects of Development," *International Development Review* (June, 1964), pp. 21–25.

42. Smith, Arthur K., Jr. "Socio-Economic Development and Political Democracy: A Causal Analysis," *Midwest Journal of Political Science,* Vol. XIII, No. 1 (Feb., 1969), pp. 95–125.

43. Smith, F. B. *The Making of the Second Reform Bill* (Cambridge, England: Cambridge University Press, 1966).

44. Thapar, Romila. *A History of India* (Baltimore: Penguin, 1966).

45. Thompson, James W. *Economic and Social History of Europe in the Later Middle Ages* (1300-1500) (New York: The Century Co., 1931).

46. Trevelyan, George M. *British History in the Nineteenth Century and After* (New York: David McKay Co., Inc., 1937).

47. White, Ralph K. and Ronald Lippitt. *Autocracy and Democracy:*

An Experimental Inquiry (New York: Harper and Brothers, 1969).

48. Wolf, Charles, Jr. "The Political Effects of Economic Programs: Some Indications from Latin America," *Economic Development and Cultural Change* (October, 1965), pp. 1–20.

49. Wood, Anthony. *Nineteenth Century Britain* (London: Longmans, 1960).

50. Zimmern, Alfred. *The Greek Commonwealth* (New York: Random House, 1956).

Comments on
"Towards a Consumption Theory of Political Democracy"

WILLIAM McCORD AND ARLINE McCORD*

In his provocative, sophisticated paper Professor Silver raises issues which should be of concern to social scientists throughout the world. If, as sociologist Seymour Lipset[1] and economist Robert Heilbronner[2] argue, economic affluence is a causal step toward political democracy, then responsible people must give up all hope for the emergence of functioning democracies in most of Africa, Asia, the Middle East, and Latin America, within the next decade. Indeed, many commentators have taken still another step. They have agreed with the Nkrumahs, the Nassers, the Sukarnos and other super-officers of this world that dictatorship may well be a necessary stage in creating the economic affluence which presumably precedes democracy.[3] The argument for a "temporary" dictatorship has its obvious attractions. Economists recognize that the exigencies of capital accumulation, the setting of priorities, and the allocation of labor may well demand a political centralization of powers. Many political scientists support this position and argue that fragile nations, created by the whims of colonial powers, must be held together by charismatic, if ruthless figures who can assure the legitimacy of the state.[4]

Sociologists, adding the weight of their speculation, often

---

* The authors are, respectively, Professor of Sociology, The City College of the City University of New York; and Assistant Professor of Sociology, Hunter College of the City University of New York.

contend that the entrenched power of land-holders or creditors, the prejudices of an indigenous population, or the greedy demands of new interest groups must be curbed by force if the economy is to develop, or a democracy is to blossom.[5]

While recognizing a gross correlation between high national income and political democracy, Professor Silver's contribution lies in his raising of the crucial question: What is the sequential nature of the relations? He outlines three alternatives: (1) A high national income may precede the blossoming of political democracy; or (2) Political democracy may pave the way for economic affluence; or (3) Both political democracy and a high national income may be the result of a "third factor."

Before discussing these alternatives, two questions should be raised: What is democracy? Professor Silver adopts Seymour Martin Lipset's definition that democracy is "a political system which supplies regular constitutional opportunities for changing the governing officials."[6] We believe that this definition does not do justice to our usual concept of democracy. Such a definition would include the Soviet Union which, *de jure*, provides constitutional opportunities for a change in governing officials and yet, *de facto*, does not allow for competing political parties. When we think of a democracy, we usually extend that concept to include certain institutional arrangements which, in the long run, are far more important than simply a constitutional agreement to allow for a circulation of elites: that is, we think of a free judiciary, a free press, protection against coercion of the masses by the ruling elite, and the provision that a change in rulers may never be carried out by force. In discussing political democracy, therefore, we would like to use a definition which encompasses these elements and describes nations as diverse as Costa Rica and Great Britain, Lebanon and Denmark. Specifically, a political democracy is most aptly defined as a system which provides for the peaceful transition of elites, guarantees freedom of the courts and the judiciary, and forbids coercion as a legitimate tactic in politics.

The concept of "high income," equally important to Professor Silver's argument, also deserves consideration. In all of the cases discussed by Professor Silver (and highlighted in the literature), an increase in income *relative* to what a particular people previously enjoyed, or *relative* to what other peoples had at the time, is usually employed. Therefore, we would argue, any attempt to correlate "high income" with political democracy must necessarily employ a concept of relative, not absolute, income. This is important for it focuses upon the subjective perception of people rather than upon the absolute measures (e.g., the number of telephones in use), which are often misleading. For example, in an absolute sense, Germany was a relatively affluent nation in the world when she succumbed to Fascism; the descent into totalitarianism took place in an atmosphere of inflation and recession which the people perceived as catastrophic. On the other hand, democracy grew vigorously in England and Scandinavia during periods of economic growth. By twentieth-century standards, however, these areas in the seventeenth and eighteenth century were abysmally poor. The crucial relationship between "high" income and political democracy, therefore, apparently depends on a people's perception of their relative wealth, rather than on absolute income.

With these attenuations in the concepts of "democracy" and "income," we may usefully turn to the three explanations which Professor Silver offers.

First, there is no substantial evidence that a relatively high national income in itself "causes" political democracy. Rather, it would appear that a population which perceives that its national income is continuously growing also exhibits a hunger for political democracy. This may well occur in contemporary Russia and Eastern Europe.

Second, there is no substantial evidence that political democracy "causes" economic affluence. In some cases, such as Denmark and Sweden, political reforms preceded a major growth in income and went hand in hand with the spread of political democracy. In still other cases, such as Costa Rica and Lebanon, democracy flourished in the absence of economic growth. And finally, in contemporary Arabic areas such as Kuwait and Saudi Arabia, affluence beyond the imagination of most men has not yet resulted in political democracy.

A third factor seems operative in governing both the growth of affluence and the spread of democracy, since they usually occur simultaneously. This elusive "third factor" seems to us to involve the following elements: (1) Democracy flourishes only when the masses believe in the *legitimacy* both of the ruling elite and of the competing claims of various secondary elites; similarly, economic growth occurs most frequently in situations where the elite fulfills both its own profit motive and those of the masses.[7] (2) A belief in the legitimacy of the ruling elite is buttressed to the degree that the regime can *fulfill* the rising economic expectations of the masses; thus, relative affluence can lead merely to the stability of an existing regime (e.g., Latin American military rulers) rather than to the growth of democracy.

A turn toward democracy occurs only when new *interest groups* (i.e., merchants, labor unions, wealthy peasants, etc.) emerge with their own bases of power *and* when growing economic affluence simultaneously satisfies the desires of the ruling elite, the new interest groups, and the masses.

These three factors—a widely held belief in the legitimacy of a regime (and of its competitors); a fulfillment of rising expectations; and the growth of interest groups with independent power—are so closely linked that it becomes impossible to extricate them. A fulfillment of rising economic expectations, for example, certainly enhances the legitimacy of a regime. Conversely, economic growth most often takes place in areas where the governing elite is sufficiently assured of its own legitimacy so that it allows competing groups to function both economically and politically. Allowing new interest groups to flourish and to gain some degree of independent political power generally insures the governing elite of the loyalty of new groups and of their continued interest in economic growth. As an economy expands, the interest groups proliferate, as does the demand for political democracy. The pattern runs in full cycle.

The elusive third factor, then, which seems to correlate with both economic affluence and the growth of political democracy, would appear to be *social pluralism*: that is, the growth of competing social groups who are independently powerful and who recognize the interests of other groups as "legitimate." When social pluralism is present (as in eighteenth-century Europe, nineteenth-century America, nineteenth-century Japan), one may expect a pattern of both economic growth and democratization. In its absence, one may find a semblance of political democracy (as in Russia) or relative economic affluence (as in China). In the absence of either social pluralism, political democracy, or relative economic affluence, one may expect that despotism and economic stagnation will be the result. Alas, this seems the fate of much of the world at the end of the twentieth century.

NOTES

1. Seymour Martin Lipset, *Political Man* (Garden City, N. Y.: Doubleday and Co., 1960).

2. Robert Heilbronner, *The Future as History* (New York: Harper and Row, 1959).

3. Paul Baran, *The Political Economy of Growth* (New York: Monthly Review Press, 1960).

4. Immanuel Wallerstein, *Africa, the Politics of Independence* (New York: Vintage Books, 1961).

5. Jdak Woddis, *Africa, the Roots of the Revolt* (London: Lawrence and Wishart, 1960).

6. Lipset, *op. cit.*

7. There are, of course, bizarre exceptions to this rule of thumb. For specific historical reasons, the rule of Nazism prompted a growth in the German national economy without an accompanying spread of democracy. Similarly, the discovery of oil in Abu Dhabi has entailed a tremendous increase in national income without bringing about either a major improvement in the welfare of the masses or the emergence of a political democracy.

7

Preliminary Thoughts about the Causes of Harmony and Conflict

MANCUR OLSON[*]

I.   What is it that holds human institutions together, when they endure, or tears them apart, when they do not? Inquiring minds must have a perennial interest in such an elemental and difficult problem as this. The interest should be particularly lively in the United States now, since it has lately been going through a period of considerable social conflict, not only in the national polity, but in cities and universities as well. Even where that most intimate institution, the nuclear family, is concerned, there is considerable uneasiness about widening generation gaps and increasing divorce rates.

Some of the concern about the threats to cohesion of society or its constituent institutions no doubt results from conservative ideology. The protests in the name of the young, the black, or of women that some see as the only sparks of hope for needed social change arouse in others fears of total chaos. It is important, however, to realize that *some* interest in social harmony and cohesion is appropriate, whatever the ideological perspective. Even if social conflict should be essential to progress, it is nonetheless costly, and thus something we would want to keep at the minimal

---

[*] Professor of Economics, University of Maryland. The author is thankful to the National Science Foundation, Resources for the Future, and the Woodrow Wilson International Center for Scholars for support of his research.

level consistent with the performance of the functions it is supposed to perform. And even if the existing society, and all of its constituent organizations, families, and other institutions, should be considered so pernicious that they were beyond repair or reform, there is still the intellectual problem of determining how any better society or institution that might be created could be preserved. Nor is a desire for a sense of community or for social cohesion inappropriate even to the classical or *laissez-faire* liberal, who is preoccupied with increasing individual liberty. Some institutional stability is needed even to preserve individual liberties. The classical liberal will usually want to attach special weight to the rights of dissent and deviance, but after some point he must also give some concern to the survival of the institutions that protect these rights.[1] From every perspective, then, the problem of social harmony is a real one.

II.   Real and ancient as the problem of harmony and conflict is, it is not well understood. This can be seen by considering two of the academically more respectable explanations of social stability and harmony that are current in this country. One of these might (albeit with some inaccuracy and unfairness) be called the "Parsonian" explanation. In vulgarized form, at least, it is used by a large proportion of American sociologists, and by some political scientists and anthropologists as well. It would take far too long to explain Parson's rich and variegated argument here, but we can casually refer, first, to one of its basic preconceptions, and, second, to one of its central conclusions.

A basic preconception of this "Parsonian" approach to cohesion and conflict, at least in its more vulgar forms, is that people usually do what they are brought up to do. As the old saying goes, the hand that rocks the cradle rules the world. Even when particular individuals are tempted to deviate from the paths of behavior that most of those in the society were brought up to follow, they are not likely to persevere in their deviance, since societies develop mechanisms of social control, ranging from informal social ostracism to formal or legal sanctions, which discourage or suppress deviance.[2] The presumption that human behavior is in large part governed by the values and (at a more specific level) norms that a society passes on from one generation to another leads most Parsonian sociologists (as well as many others) to give special emphasis to the process of socialization in a society and in the cultural groups within it.

One of the central conclusions derived from the foregoing presumption is, of course, that the stability or harmony of a society depends notably on the common pattern of socialization in that society, because this common pattern creates a large measure of consensus about the most basic matters, at least, and with this general agreement there is no reason for serious social conflict, or any danger of collapse of the society or the political system. Parsonian sociologists tend to explain why socialization creating similar values and sentiments leads to consensus and social stability, and (as is commonly pointed out) are a good deal less explicit about why there should be conflict, change, or collapse. Nonetheless, it is implicit in their thinking and sometimes explicitly stated, that divergent values, presumably resulting because diverse patterns of socialization somehow emerged, lead to conflict and loss of the sense of community.[3] The idea that similar values lead to social harmony and stability goes back long before Parsons, but the single-minded elaboration of this point is also distinctly Parsonian. Parsons has, for example, tended to belittle Emile Durkheim's notion that some part of social cohesion arose because of the "organic solidarity" arising from the division of labor, and instead emphasized the greater centrality of Durkheim's other concept of "mechanical solidarity," which results from the collective conscience or similar values in a society.[4]

The second of the two well-known explanations of solidarity and conflict that needs to be mentioned here is that which explains the unity of any group or society in terms of the threats that group or society perceives from external forces. The notion that the unity of a collectivity increases when its members perceive an external threat is part of the common coin of popular discussion. It therefore need not be related here to any body of scientific literature, as enlightening as a survey of the work of Georg Simmel,[5] L. A. Coser,[6] and others might be. The notion that the unity of a group increases when it perceives an outside enemy has often figured prominently in authoritative discussions of public policy, as when a member of Abraham Lincoln's cabinet advised him to provoke a war with England in hopes of preventing the American civil war.[7] Though the motives behind policies are obscure, this idea must have actually affected practical policy in many cases.

III. The sources of harmony and conflict cannot be understood without considering some differences in the nature of the objectives people seek. All human objectives may be classified as either "divisible" or "indivisible." An objective is divisible if it is such that it can be achieved for one individual, without thereby bringing about the same state of affairs for others (or by directly affecting others' production functions or utility functions[8]). Divisible objectives are achieved in either of two ways: 1) by isolated individual actions only, or 2) by individual action which is combined with or interdependent with the action of others. An indivisible objective, by contrast, is an objective such that it cannot be attained for a single individual without thereby *directly*[9] changing the state of affairs for some group of individuals. Commonly the changed state of affairs will involve a common interest or objective for everyone in the group, so that its achievement benefits all, but an objective is also defined as indivisible even if it is held by only one individual, if attaining that objective has a direct (nonpecuniary) effect on others (who may not share the common interest in the given objective, or who may feel the impact of some other, distinct phenomenon as a side effect of the achievement of an objective for other individuals). An objective may be indivisible through either of two causes: 1) a property of nature or the known technology, which creates an inherent indivisibility, or 2) a political decision, social custom, or social choice rule that creates an indivisibility by institutional practice in a situation in which it would be physically or technologically possible to have divisibility.[10]

These classifications may not immediately prove to be intuitively meaningful until they have been related to actual examples and used in the argument for which they are designed. The basic distinction between divisible and indivisible objectives is, however, the same as the distinction, in some definitional systems, between private or individual and public or collective goods. The language of "indivisibility" has been used in place of that of "publicness" to make it more obvious that *all* human objectives (however intangible or "uneconomic") involve either collective or private goods, to avoid some confusions arising from differences in the definition of collective goods,[11] and to underline the point that externalities are included and are indeed analytically identical to other collective goods.

We begin, then, with examples of divisible objectives which have been achieved only by isolated individual action. Obviously, in the modern, interdependent society in which we live, only a very few objectives are in fact attained through purely individual action which has no impact on other individuals. If a person is troubled by an itch, and cures the itch by scratching himself, he has achieved a divisible objective by purely individual action, and in a way in which no other individual's welfare need have been affected. Some psychological or spiritual purposes which call for solitude, and some kinds of artistic or esthetic efforts designed only for the one who made the effort, would fall in the same category. Other modern examples could be found, but not many.

In the most primitive stages of human history, it is much easier to think of divisible objectives achieved through isolated action alone. In periods when the technology was so primitive that man lived by food gathering, or spearing fish with a pointed stick, one can imagine some individuals often satisfying their objectives through isolated efforts which involved no interdependence with anyone else.

Obviously, in any situation in which all objectives were divisible, and achieved solely through isolated action having no interdependence with others, no problem of social conflict or harmony arises. There is, by definition, no social interaction, and no society, group, or institution which could exhibit harmony or be troubled by conflict.

IV. Let us next consider instances in which divisible objectives are best obtained through interdependence with others. If we change our perspective from the hypothetical individual in totally primitive, isolated conditions to that of, say, a farmer in the United States in the last century, we immediately presume that the farmer can best meet his needs for food, clothing, tools and the like by specializing in the raising of things which he can raise with relative efficiency (things in which he has a comparative advantage), and then bartering or selling his specialized commodities in return for other things he needs, but which he can not so efficiently provide for himself. The farmer may care about no one but himself, and share no common purposes with anyone, yet find it expedient to enter into interdependence with others by exchanging values with them.

Now suppose that the farmer should have not only material objectives, but also the objective of sexual relations, and want a wife, a mistress, or a prostitute. His objectives might be thoroughly personal, involving no sharing of purposes with anyone. Yet he could achieve them only through inter-dependence with one or more other persons. This inter-dependence could, however, well arise without his finding any woman who shared his interest in sex: he might obtain the sexual satisfaction he sought through an exchange, whereby he might provide a woman a home and livelihood, or presents, or even money, in return for the sexual liaison he desired. (There is no suggestion here, by the way, that the institutions of marriage and the family, or the relation-ship between the sexes, are adequately explained in these simple terms. Nonetheless, everyday language suggests that marriage is often thought of partly as an exchange, not only in those cultures with dowries, bride prices, and the like, but also in our society. We rarely see a marriage between a stupid, ugly, poor person of low status, and an intelligent, attractive, rich person of high status. And whenever we do, it is described as unequal. And many people speak of women who have married "well," "badly," "up," and "down.") What is the nature of this interdependence, in-volving exchanges in pursuit of divisible objectives? And what does it have to do with harmony and conflict?

The central feature of this interdependence is that it is, in the absence of force, fraud, or mistake, *mutually ad-vantageous*.[12] If one of the parties to an exchange had thought the transaction would have led to an undesirable or disadvantageous result, he would not have participated. This mutual advantage must surely encourage social har-mony, and perhaps also a concern to protect the institutions that facilitate the mutually advantageous transactions. There can, of course, be interdependence which is not mutually advantageous, and which leads to social conflict, as we shall see later, but this interdependence does not consist of ex-change. The interdependence that arises through exchange, in the absence of force, fraud, or mistake, is always mutually advantageous, and thus to some extent at least surely pro-ductive of social harmony. This applies to exchanges of the marital type as well as those involving material goods, labor, or services, and holds true however much monopoly or inequality there may be in the system. (There are, to be sure, many considerations that limit the applicability of what has just been said, but these considerations all fit under the heading of "indivisible objectives" which will be treated later. Divisible and indivisible objectives have been defined in such a way that all possible substantial arguments that criticize, or limit the applicability of what has just been said, come under the latter heading.)

One implication of the analysis so far is that, as self-subsistence declines and exchange becomes more advantageous, social and institutional integration should tend to increase, since the extent of mutually advantageous interaction increases. Also, as improvements in transportation and communication or other factors make long distance trade more advantageous, the maximum size of a harmonious social institution can increase. (Many other factors are of course also relevant in explaining the maximum feasible scale of governments or other institutions, some of which probably have more quantitative importance than the point that has just been made. This point is nonetheless relevant, and in some cases probably important as well.)

Another implication of the analysis so far is that the Parsonian conclusion that social cohesion rests on similar values, resulting from common patterns of socialization, is unsatisfactory. If individuals have similar tastes in consumption, and all want to do the same kind of work, the gains from exchanges among them will be less than if they had different values. Clearly, people with identical wants, skills, and resources will gain nothing from trade with each other, and therefore are without an important incentive for social harmony. If, by contrast, they either want to consume different things, or desire to produce different things, they will tend to gain from exchange. Because the Germans like sausage, and the French demand the better cuts, there has been an advantageous meat trade between the two countries. If everyone wants a vacation in August at the beach, there is expensive congestion there at vacation time, and a lack of basic services elsewhere (this is a problem that has received official attention in France). But if some want a vacation in winter instead, or prefer to go to the mountains, everyone can be better off. If some want to work outdoors and others indoors, there will be more job satisfaction than there would be otherwise, provided only that free exchange of the output of men in different occupations is allowed. A common market involving the diverse nations of Western Europe can possibly prove advantageous and unifying, whereas a common market among the Arab nations (though often supported) makes much less sense (they can't usefully export oil to each other, but can advantageously trade with industrialized economies).

This point about the virtues of diversity is by no means related only to trade in material goods. One does not maximize Motherhood by bringing women together. If one marriage partner likes fat, and the other lean, they can together lick the platter clean. A marriage is more likely to be successful if one of the partners wants to lead, and the other wants to follow, than if both have the same desire. A similar point can be made about any organization. If different leaders or countries want different objectives, they will often be able to resolve disputes to their mutual advantage, but if both Princes want Milan, or both Germanies want Berlin, the problem is more difficult to resolve without conflict. It is, in short, wrong to argue, as many do, that similar values or consensus is what holds a society or group together.

V.   Indivisible objectives were defined as objectives such that, if achieved for an individual, they also directly change the state of affairs for one or more other individuals (or for an entire society). If a given indivisible objective is achieved for some individual or group, no other individual in the relevant group, or no other group in the relevant society, can be excluded from benefiting when this objective is achieved, if they share it; or opt out, if they don't; or avoid some distinct side effect, if there is one. A familiar example of an indivisible objective is defense. If a nation's military establishment deters other nations from attacking, everyone who lives in the defended nation is protected— even the pacifists, who don't want to be. Another indivisible objective is control of pollution. If the air over New York is cleaned up for one, it is cleaned up for all. For a married couple, the number of children they will have, or the nature of the house they will live in, are indivisible objectives, as both must put up with the same outcome. For Catholics, papal leadership is an indivisible objective, since there must be only one Pope for them all. For the world as a whole, the level of pure or basic scientific research is an indivisible objective, since we all share the consequences of the discovery of new, general knowledge.

Just as exchange has tended to become relatively more important over time, in relation to isolation and self-subsistence, so it seems likely that in *recent* decades, indivisible objectives have become relatively more important as compared with divisible ones. Whereas the interdependence of the nineteenth-century farmer was mainly felt through the market, the contemporary city dweller is interdependent in another way as well. He shares with most others in the city the indivisible objectives relating to the limitation of pollution, congestion, noise, and crime. He also shares with most others in the city the objectives of a more attractive cityscape, better parks, a faster flow of traffic, and so on. There usually is a good deal of disagreement about exactly how a city should be changed, but there is no denying the indivisibility, i.e., the fact that everyone in the city must live with the same changes. Similarly, the growing relative importance of science and basic research, and the special urgency of international relations in this shrinking and thermonuclear world, also argue that indivisible objectives are becoming more important. It is evident, at least, that the proportionate role of governments, which deal mainly with indivisible objectives, is increasing over time in all or almost all of the countries that are industrialized or enjoying economic advance.

As I have argued elsewhere,[13] it is normally (though definitely not always) the case that large groups can attain indivisible objectives (which are also called collective or public goods) only through coercion.[14] If the foregoing argument about the growing relative importance of indivisible objectives is correct, it follows that there may well be a tendency for the use of coercion to increase over time. The fact that the attainment of indivisible objectives for larger groups normally requires coercion also has important implications for social harmony and conflict, as we shall now see.

It is probably true that most people do not like to be subject to the use of force, or to be influenced by threats. Since indivisible objectives for large groups normally require force or threats of force, such objectives are a likely cause of conflict.

More importantly, indivisible objectives are achieved for none or achieved for all in the relevant group and to the same extent. If a nation has a militant foreign policy, the benefits and hazards of this foreign policy have the same objective impact on every citizen. Whatever defense budget a nation chooses, both the militarists and the pacifists must put up with it. When the air over a city is polluted, everyone must accept the existing effort to combat pollution and the existing level of pollution, whatever they might prefer. In a family, both husband and wife must accept the same decision about how many children to have, or what house to live in.

What this means is that indivisible objectives are a source of conflict when the affected individuals have different wants or values. That is what explains the element of truth in the Parsonian sociological proposition that consensus is one source of social harmony and stability. For maximal harmony, the people in an institution or society should have diverse values with respect to divisible objectives and like values with respect to indivisible values or collective goods. Though this point has not been properly understood by modern writers, there is, as critics of my argument have correctly pointed out, something vaguely like it in Durkheim's classical distinction between "organic" and "mechanical" solidarity.

With the aid of the concept of indivisible objectives or collective goods, which Durkheim could hardly have known, we can also examine the familiar notion that a group obtains unity through perception of an external threat. Though there is a degree of truth in this notion, it can be seriously misleading. The degree of truth stems from the possibility that, when a group perceives a serious threat from without, it may, if the threat and the way to deal with it are sufficiently obvious, unite in meeting that threat. Combatting the threat is an indivisible objective of the group. If the threat is sufficiently serious, and the appropriate way of dealing with it obvious enough, it may make other indivisible objectives, about which there is disagreement, relatively insignificant, thereby increasing unity.

Often, however, the threat will not be perceived in the same way by everyone in the group. What is a threat to some is a blessing, or a matter of indifference, to others. Even where there is agreement on the nature of the threat, there may be disagreement about the best strategy for dealing with it. Thus, a real or alleged threat to a group can cause social division as well as solidarity. There is no lack of examples of this point. The United States has, since shortly after World War II, perceived a threat from Communism. But this perceived threat has by no means brought unity; indeed, McCarthyism, and controversies over the Korean and Vietnamese wars, which would not have occurred but for this perceived threat, have been leading sources of social division. Similarly, France perceived a threat from Germany before and during World War II. Yet this threat hardly succeeded in keeping the country unified. The French could not agree on whether to capitulate or on how to combat the threat.

VI.   The initial classification of objectives pointed out that some objectives were indivisible because of properties of nature or technology, whereas others were indivisible only because of prevailing institutional practice. The examples of indivisibilities that have been cited so far are all of the former type. Consider now an objective that is indivisible simply because of certain institutional arrangements. Suppose the provision of housing is handled through the government, with the construction and maintenance of housing paid for out of general tax revenues and housing provided free to citizens. There are inefficiencies in such an arrangement that are made clear in every elementary economics text.[15] One disadvantage that is not usually mentioned is the likelihood that such an arrangement will increase conflict. If housing is provided as a collective good, rather than through the market, the society as a unit must decide how much to spend on housing and what kind of housing to provide. Some prefer a large percentage of resources to go to housing; others only a small percentage. And tastes in what the housing should be like are almost infinitely varied. Thus *any* collective decision about housing is likely to prove unsatisfactory to many people, and therefore divisive. In general, when any divisible objective is made indivisible through a collectivization process,[16] the sources of conflict will be increased. We can, then, see that the analysis has a normative implication, which is that social conflict can be lessened by avoiding the bureaucratic provision of goods that would otherwise be divisible.[17]

It might be argued that in making a private good indivisible the consumers will gain through what Albert Hirschman has labeled "voice" (participation in decision-making) what they have lost through the disappearance of what he calls "exit" (the right not to purchase). But this is not correct, and involves a far too common misunderstanding of the relation between voice and exit. Unless somehow everyone has exactly the same tastes, no system for giving individuals voice can give them either the welfare or the exemption from conflict that could have been attained had the good been left divisible.[18] With an ideal majority-vote democratic system, for example, the subgroups in a majority coalition will argue on the level and type of housing, and impose this and a corresponding tax-expenditure pattern on the minority, who will normally prefer something different. Even most of those in the majority will not obtain just what they want, or would have chosen had divisibility been retained; a single common decision must replace the separate choices of the diverse individuals involved. Thus the value of the voice gained will be less than the value of the exit lost, and in addition the occasions for conflict increased, by the introduction of a gratuitous indivisibility.

A second normative implication of the model is that *appropriate* decentralization of *certain* functions of government can increase social harmony. Many problems, such as air and water pollution, are different in each area. If the efforts to deal with these problems are solely at a national level, programs are not likely to take into account differences among areas in the policy desired, or possibly even differences in the extent of the problem. Appropriate decentralization can then make it possible for more people to have the policy they want than would be the case under national provision.

The values relating to some collective goods, especially police protection, education, parks, and swimming pools, vary among racial, ethnic, and income groups. Many people prefer policemen and teachers with backgrounds akin to their own. If there is racial segregation, or any other force creating ghettos, then the people in different neighborhoods tend to have different cultural backgrounds. The different neighborhoods or ghettos accordingly often want different types of collective goods, or different levels of provision and taxation. I have elsewhere[19] developed an argument which endeavors to show that there is a need, in terms of static economic efficiency, for "fiscal equivalence," or a separate jurisdiction for every collective good or indivisible objective with a unique boundary. This principle requires separate jurisdictions for ghettos or neighborhoods which want different types of collective goods. If the argument here is correct, fiscal equivalence also has the advantage of minimizing social conflict, at least in the short run. In the long run, to be sure, the unity and well-being of a society may be increased by forcing different groups to put up with the same collective goods, on the theory that they will then all grow accustomed to the same thing. Thus we can not go directly from this model alone to practical policy. But however many considerations might be relevant, and whatever the best choice on balance, it is important to keep the case for fiscal equivalence as a strategy of social harmony in mind.

It is difficult to attempt to relate the insights of literary men to an economic argument, but it is nonetheless probable that Norman Mailer's desire to make New York City the fifty-first state, and his argument that each neighborhood community should have some degree of autonomous government, could be explained in terms of the concepts set out here. When Mailer argued that it would be desirable to have some communities where free love was compulsory, and other communities where church attendance was compulsory, he was for making some divisible objectives indivisible, and therefore countering the sense of community he sought. But the idea of neighborhood jurisdictions dealing with problems largely peculiar to the neighborhood is the same as that which emerges from the model of fiscal equivalence and the arguments developed here.

VII. At the international or comparative politics level, the argument that has just been made implies that empires or large states would on occasion break into smaller units, and that some or all of the peoples involved might gain from this, if the larger empire did not have a federal structure with responsive smaller jurisdictions that could meet distinct local problems. Since, as we argued with respect to "ghetto" populations, separate cultural traditions normally entail distinct tastes for collective goods (and especially those that are symbols of a group's pride or self-esteem), "national" cultural differences naturally often also lead to demands for separate nations. As Stein Rokkan has most notably pointed out, a distinct language, and especially an elite using that language and producing literature with it, can provide the basis for a distinct political development and, of course, for the breakup of large polyglot empires. A common language is, of course, a collective good to those who know it, and it is used to socialize children and to transmit cultural symbols, so it is by no means surprising in terms of the model here that the organizing principle of so many nation-states is language, and that there are fissiparous tendencies, decentralized federal structures, or strong totalitarian systems, in all multi-lingual states.

Though the present argument has focused on the conflict-avoiding virtues of decentralization, it is important to remember that the principle of fiscal equivalence also argues that there are losses in efficiency or effectiveness from a lack of sufficiently encompassing jurisdictions for the provision of collective goods with a large domain or "catchment area." Indeed, since pure research, the suppression of violence among major powers, and protection of the oceans, for example, are world-wide public goods, there are demonstrable difficulties that arise from the lack of a meaningful world-wide jurisdiction. Thus at the same time that objective local problems and cultural differences create demands for local or regional jurisdictions, there are demands, especially (as would be predicted) among small countries, for stronger international organizations, for "common market"-size jurisdictions, and so on.

It would take us beyond the scope of the present paper to go into the question of what would be the most promising approach to world-wide international organizations, and/or to institutions of the common market type. Yet it is clear that the theory of collective goods as it is understood in this paper, when combined with the principle of fiscal equivalence, offers a framework for analyzing these questions in a way that they are not normally analyzed, either by my fellow economists or by scientists in other fields. It would be possible to ask, for example, whether the early progress of the Common Market was not due in part to the diversity of its member peoples and the magnitude of the trade barriers that then existed, and which the common market was initially able to lower for trade among its member states. As trade barriers generally perhaps became lower through the Kennedy Round and other developments, and (more importantly) as the Common Market has come to the stage where "political coordination" or the production of public goods has become more important, the Common Market seems to have lost some of its integrative momentum. There are many reasons, but is it not possible that the diversity that made integration through trade advantageous is making political coordination more difficult?

VIII. The rough and ready outline of a model that has just been presented leaves out many important aspects of the great problem of social and political cohesion. A complete discussion would have to deal with the charisma, or lack of it, of leaders, the expectations and psychology of the population, the mechanisms for resolving disputes, and many other factors. Most important of all, the determinants of differences among societies, institutions, and periods in the degree of conflict about the distribution of income and welfare need to be included. Every society faces the "problem" of allocating its total output among the individuals in the society through one social process or another. Since this problem is always present, at least at the level of society as a whole, it cannot explain why some societies cohere whereas others are torn asunder. Yet the *intensity* of disputes over distribution can obviously make a difference, and a complete theory would need to take account of whatever factors determine variations in this. Thus we are a long way from a conceptually complete model of harmony and conflict. Yet when such a comprehensive model is developed, it will surely have to include the distinction between divisible and indivisible objectives and the very different roles they play in the generation of conflict and cooperation.

NOTES

1. For an analysis that brings out the inevitability of the trade-off between individual liberty and social cohesion, see U.S. Department of Health, Education, and Welfare, *Toward a Social Report* (U.S. Government Printing Office, Washington, D. C. 20407, 1969), Chapter 7 on "Participation and Alienation."

2. One mechanism of social control Parsonian sociologists have cited is the mechanism of isolation, whereby potentially conflicting elements are isolated. This mechanism of social control can prevent conflict without achieving consensus. I am thankful to Richard Derr for help on this point.

3. This casual sentence does not do justice to the patient historical and statistical research that some Parsonian sociologists have devoted to the question of social conflict, and to the diverse insights they have gained. See, for example, Neil Smelser's book on *Social Change in the Industrial Revolution* (Chicago, Illinois: University of Chicago Press, 1959) and the conflict, change, and structural differentiation that were inherent in it.

4. See Parson's most interesting, if ultimately unsatisfactory,

article on "Durkheim's Contribution to the Theory of Integration of Social Systems" in Kurt H. Wolff, ed., *Essays in Sociology and Philosophy* (New York: Harper Torchbooks, 1964), pp. 118-53, and his monumental *Structure of Social Action*, 2nd. ed. (New York: The Free Press, 1949), pp. 301-42.

5. See Georg Simmel, *Conflict and the Web of Group Affiliations*, Kurt Wolff and Reinhard Bendix, trans. (Glencoe, Illinois: The Free Press, 1950), and *The Sociology of Georg Simmel*, Kurt Wolff, trans. (Glencoe, Illinois: The Free Press, 1950).

6. L. A. Coser, *The Functions of Social Conflict* (Glencoe, Illinois: The Free Press, 1956).

7. To which suggestion Lincoln aptly replied "one war at a time."

8. What Pigou called "pecuniary externalities"—actions which affect prices, and thus the quantities of goods that are taken, but do not *directly* impinge on production functions or utility levels—are consistent with a divisible good.

9. Again, changes in relative prices, such as will occur from almost any action in a general equilibrium system, do not make an objective indivisible; they involve merely pecuniary externalities.

10. In some cases it is readily possible to make an objective divisible, but socially inefficient to do so, because the objective has the property that if achieved for one or some, it is socially costless to provide it to others, or can in any event be provided to others at a marginal social cost less than the average per capita cost. These cases will very often lead to indivisibility by institutional practice.

11. Note that what John Head calls "jointness"—the decreasing-cost type of public good—is here defined to involve a collectiveness or indivisibility only when there is also nonexclusion, either through nature or institutional practice.

12. To be sure, the point that market exchange is mutually beneficial and thus conducive to social harmony, is very old. It has lately been stated with a wealth of interesting detail in Jan Pen, *Harmony and Conflict in Modern Society*, Trevor S. Preston, trans. (New York: McGraw Hill, 1966).

13. Mancur Olson, *The Logic of Collective Action* (Cambridge, Mass.: Harvard University Press, 1965; paperback, Schocken Books, 1968).

14. The behavior that can be induced by threat can also be induced by rewards if a source of rewards exists.

15. However, if the heretofore divisible good has "jointness" so that new consumers did not reduce the amount consumed by the old consumers, or decreasing costs generally, then making it indivisible could increase efficiency.

16. If firms are collectivized, but continue to operate in response to market signals, there is no need for collectivization to increase conflict.

17. It may sometimes be the case that a problem with divisible goods is so frustrating that people say, "Don't just stand there, do something." Then government action might be unifying in the short run, even if it converted a divisible good into a collective good.

18. Again the case of jointness or decreasing costs is left aside.

19. Mancur Olson, "The Principle of Fiscal Equivalence," *American Economic Review Proceedings* (May, 1969).

Comments on
"Preliminary Thoughts about the Causes of Harmony and Conflict"

Manoucher Parvin[*]

I. INTRODUCTION

Professor Olson argues for the relevance and importance of economic models in explaining social harmony or conflict; he also suggests the usefulness of sociological insights and models in explaining economic behavior such as consumption. He does not, however, define or describe the nature or extent of potential conflicts and their probable mode or forms of manifestation. Obviously, conflicts resulting in violence are qualitatively different from those resulting in a social debate and dissipated or resolved in process. If the basic contention of this work is accepted, it becomes self-evident that the nature and scope of such conflicts are histo-economically relative. Historical and economic specificities determine the forms and dimension of conflicts and thus their potential harms and costs. Thus, further transformation of divisible objectives to indivisible ones may increase or decrease conflict depending on time, place or cultural characteristic of a society.

I am in complete sympathy and agreement with Professor Olson's argument that conflict or cohesion are inadequately explained by the force of a value structure in a social unit.

---

[*] Assistant Professor of Economics, Hunter College of the City University of New York. (The author is now Associate Professor of Economics, Fordham University.)

180

Even if the Parsonian approach was accepted, it could not explain how fixed values can resolve contradictions arising from a rapidly changing society. New values would be required to cope with new situations and thus, the need for such painful transformations would create conflict within or between individuals and among larger social units. However, the literature of conflict resolution is rich with works by biologists, psychologists, political scientists, sociologists, economists, and prophets. Professor Olson chooses to disregard this accumulated treasure of man's reflection on man's cruelty to humankind.[1] Furthermore, I disagree with the adopted methodology, with certain assumptions made, with explanatory factors chosen, and associated logical and/or normative conclusions reached.

II. DISCUSSION

All human objectives are classified into two categories of "divisible" or "indivisible" goods which are a generalization of private and public goods, including externalities, etc. However, this traditional division is more conceptual than actual. Although all people have equal "rights" to attend a Shakespeare play in Central Park, the proximity to the park, the private wealth in terms of human capital, determining taste, availability of leisure time, and other objective factors affect the exercise of such rights which are not all voluntary. Furthermore, there are only a few truly "private" consumption activities left. Thus, the closer geographical, technological, and social connectedness has resulted in greater interdependence and thus the merging of the two goods. For example, while the use of a specific location of a public beach by an individual is *private* for a period of time the construction activity on one's land is partially a *public* activity due to the interference of zoning rules and regulations. In light of Professor Olson's own admission to such historical convergence of the two forms in which human objectives are manifested, it is difficult to see how this division could be considered as an important cause of conflict.

The properties of divisibility and indivisibility are used to derive the following conclusion: "For maximal harmony, the people in an institution or society should have diverse values with respect to divisible objectives and like values with respect to indivisible values or collective goods." This important conclusion is obtained by examples which can be invalidated by equally good counterexamples. For instance, given budgetary constraints, when a husband and wife are choosing between alternatives of a hifi set or a trip, a conflict may arise. The formation of monopoly by oil-producing countries contradicts Olson's hypothesis that conflict, rather than cooperation, is a likely occurrence for countries with like values. In these cases, and numerous similar examples, the *diverse values* are a cause of conflict in institutions and *like values*, a catalyst for peace and harmony. Furthermore, if a large number of people had like values to bathe in a given beach or attend Shakespeare's Festival, conflict would result due to overcrowding. Such contradictions in Olson's proposition can be resolved if we add what I would call Parvin's Principle. Prior to resource allocation, like values by members of a social unit cause a harmonious achievement of the objectives, while, *a posteriori*, diverse values result in avoidance of potential conflict. So, for the future flow of divisible or indivisible objectives, like values by decision-makers help the cause of peace, while diverse values for use of existing goods or already achieved objectives, dry the fuel of potential war. This statement contradicts the entire argument of Olson, since it finds no difference between divisible or indivisible goods insofar as social harmony and conflict are concerned.

One important normative conclusion of Professor Olson is ". . . that social conflict can be lessened by avoiding the bureaucratic provision of goods that would otherwise be divisible. . . ." He relies on problems associated with public housing to support the above principle. However, if public housing causes movement toward optimum distribution of income insofar as social harmony is concerned, then the net effect, in spite of bureaucratic interference, could be favorable.[2]

Two important questions are here unnecessarily mixed. One is the question of optimum level of equality (or inequality) in the income distribution, and the other the optimum centralization (or decentralization) of social activity arrangement. Such optimal levels (for minimizing potential or actual conflict) are historically related entities. The optimum levels may vary from one social unit to another or within the same unit over time. Professor Olson seems to be biased toward decentralization as such, at least in certain categories of activities, without addressing the general question of situation-related optimum centralization insofar as economic productivity or, what I would call peace productivity, is concerned.

As far as methodology and logic are concerned, a counter-example can negate a general hypothesis, but numerous supporting examples cannot substantiate a positive statement. So, although I have at least some reservation about each individual example offered, even if one would agree with all such examples, the method of study here would still be considered inadequate.

III. CONCLUSION

Finally, it is not so much the nature of goods (divisibility and indivisibility) which is a cause of conflict, but rather, the process of "objective" selection and the distribution of such objectives. Thus, concerning the contribution of economic factors to social harmony or disharmony, the important questions are not how objectives are provided (public or private), but if they are provided at all and how they are distributed. A man desiring food, housing, education or medical attention cares more if he receives any (or if others receive it and he does not), than in which form the objectives are provided—public or private. Accordingly, the crucial conflict-creating (or diminishing) factors such as the absolute or relative present and/or expected level of deprivation, growth of objective availability (e.g., income growth rate), social mobility, discrimination, communication, social consciousness heightening, etc., are missing without explanation. Hence, only the secondary questions of economic causes of social conflict are handled in a rather inadequate manner in this preliminary work. However, Professor Olson must be credited for directing his intellectual energies toward the question of economic explanation of social conflict—a very important problem.

NOTES

1. Terry Maple and Douglas W. Matheson, eds., *Aggression, Hostility and Violence: Nature or Nurture?* (New York: Holt, Rinehart, and Winston, Inc., 1973).

2. Manoucher Parvin, "Economic Determinants of Political Unrest: An Econometric Approach," *Journal of Conflict Resolution* (June, 1973).

8

Some Economic Determinants of the Characteristics of Public Workers

R. D. AUSTER*

Public policy, public work, is carried out by people. Public workers are needed to produce public goods[1] and we cannot simply assume that these individuals acting in their own interests will be led to make decisions and take actions which are of optimal benefit to society as a whole. Public workers need correct incentives, and must be capable individuals suited to their employment if the public is to be well served. Jobs requiring keen insight into the course of future events are unlikely to be performed adequately by individuals with low intelligence; a pacifist would make a poor executioner. Who will be called to public work?

If we accept the traditional economic assumption that individuals choose their jobs in a way which maximizes their own expected utility, then certain jobs will of necessity be more attractive to certain types of people. Risk averters, for example, will tend to avoid selecting occupations associated with high levels of risk, while individuals who dislike physical exertion will try to avoid occupations requiring strenuous physical effort. In general, every job can be described by a vector of its characteristics,[2] while each

* Associate Professor of Economics, University of Arizona. This draft has benefited from the comments of J. L. Barr, D. G. Heckerman, B. Sears, M. Silver, G. Sirkin, V. Tabbush, G. Tullock and J. Wenders on earlier drafts and the spirited comments of the conference participants. Responsibility remains mine.

individual has a utility function which depends on his experience of these characteristics and various other variables.
The associated wage or salary is simply one of the characteristics of any particular job; others are such things as
the number of hours one is required to attend to the job,
non-pecuniary characteristics such as status, stress, risk, the
extent of opportunity for theft and more general shirking,
etc.[3] Given its levels of the various characteristics other than
wage or salary relative to other available jobs, any particular
job will tend to attract various types of persons in a predictable manner. Individuals with less intense dislikes (or
greater likes) for characteristics of a job, other than wage
or salary, will be willing to accept a lower wage and thus
ceteris paribus will be hired first. Alternatively, if the wage
is considered a given, individuals who place more emphasis
on the job's other characteristics will be willing to expend
more effort in acquiring it, and thus will be more likely
to succeed in doing so.[4] *Ceteris paribus*, people choose
jobs so as to maximize their "specific rents."

What, then, are the special characteristics of public employments in general and of the job of politician in particular?[5] Assuming there are such characteristics, we should be
able to use the foregoing analysis to predict what types of
people will seek public employment, to discern whether
or not such people are likely to be able to function effectively, and perhaps to see how such jobs might be restruc-
tured to attract persons more compatible with their function.

While we propose to discuss public workers in general,
both politicians and civil servants, we do not mean to
suggest that these groups possess exactly the same characteristics. The jobs differ with respect to the relative levels
of some characteristics, but not others, and thus the individuals called to the jobs will differ. These differences in
the characteristics of politicians and civil servants are analyzed and shown to have predictable consequences for
public policy.[6]

I. THE SPECIAL CHARACTERISTICS OF PUBLIC EMPLOYMENT AND THE CONSEQUENT CHARACTERISTICS OF PUBLIC WORKERS

Public employments in general, and in particular the job of politician, are characterized by a relatively large opportunity to advance the public good, and a relatively high degree of job certainty which results mainly from the civil service system but also from a system which always rewards loyal, long-term work for a political party or political machine. The specific job of politician does, however, have greater job uncertainty than other public employments. In addition, public employment is characterized by a certain amount of power, that is, the ability to coerce others (affect them without prior consent), and large opportunities for shirking [5, 8]. We proceed to analyze the consequences of each of these characteristics in turn.

A. The Public Good

Because of the very nature of any public job, there are often opportunities to advance the public good or, more generally, to alter actual public policy for the better. This opportunity is rarely large except in certain key positions, but it is, by definition, always present to a greater degree than in priavte jobs. Unfortunately, as we have shown elsewhere [2], the improvement in one's well-being through the increased level of the public good is generally irrelevant to an individual's choice of a course of action unless he is important to the outcome (or believes himself to be so) or he views the issues as one of overwhelming importance (that is, failure to adopt a specific policy, or achieve a specific level of public good, is viewed as an infinite disaster). This follows immediately from the fact that, because it is public, the good will be obtained by the individual in any case, so that how much good there is (or will be) must be irrelevant to the individual's choices. The classic free-rider problem is always present for public workers.

Individuals, then, will generally seek public employment
for the opportunity to advance the public good it provides
only if they believe they will be important to the outcome
or if they view some issue as of overwhelming importance.
In the vast, diffuse bureaucracies which seem to typify
public employment, few jobs can realistically be viewed as
important to overall public outcomes. In those few jobs
with real power, such as some political, military, and appointed positions, the individual should have recognized
initially the low probability of his being chosen for the
position. Thus, only those whose views of the consequences
of alternate public policies are impassioned and perhaps
unrealistic, or those who hold strangely optimistic views
of the probability of their achieving high public office, will
be attracted to public work by the desire to see the public
good advanced.[7] These characteristics are more likely to be
present for politicians, because of the closer connection of
their work with the level of public good.

On the other hand, it cannot be denied that some people
derive satisfaction from acting in what they believe to be
the public interest itself—patriots do exist.[8] They are attracted to public work, not by the desire to see the public
good advanced, but rather by the desire to support that
advancement irrespective of whether or not it is achieved.[9]
Thus, public employment, particularly those positions with
some real opportunities for improving the public good, will
tend to attract the patriotic; those with an unusually large,
perhaps inflated, sense of their own historical importance
(or luck); and those who hold extreme views about the
consequences of alternative policies.

Patriots are extremely valuable, but only to the extent
that they correctly perceive the correct policy, and only
to the extent that they do not desire action for its own sake.
The other two types would seem to be dangerous people to
trust with the power usually associated with important

public jobs. Their attitudes or expectations exhibit some signs of imbalance.

B. Risk

Largely as a result of the existence of a civil service system, but also because of the lower variability, especially in the downward direction, of the revenue available to support employees, which results from the "market power" of governments, public work as a whole tends to be characterized by large amounts of job certainty. Because of this, such work is certain to attract generally risk-averse individuals. This may have unfortunate consequences for the quality of government policy because such individuals are very unlikely to wish to see change of any sort, since change necessarily brings with it an increased level of uncertainty. Reluctance to change will have especially unfortunate consequences if the social order should begin to change more rapidly.

Politicians, as well as key officials, however, are likely to be exceptions to this general risk aversiveness among public workers. By the very fact that they are politicians we know that at one point in their lives they were willing to invest considerable resources in an endeavor which generally has an uncertain outcome. They ran for public office for the first time. From this we can infer that they once were not entirely risk averse, but this inference is only strictly correct if politicians pay for their own campaigns and if there is genuine uncertainty about the outcomes of elections. Neither is the case when there is a strong political machine. Where, however, there is in effect only one party, as was the case throughout the south after the Civil War, then primary elections (implicit or explicit) become the election, and we again have the presumption that politicians are likely not to be entirely risk averse. Thus, only when others pay for one's campaign is this basic conclusion modified. This is unlikely to be true when one runs for one's first office.

The politician in most instances does run some risk of losing (or having to change) jobs periodically as the typical bueaucrat does not, except for those upper-level bureaucrats whose positions are not civil service, e.g., upper-echelon decision-makers such as the Secretary of State. The conclusion that politicians and upper-echelon bureaucrats will be less risk averse than the general civil servants who will be required to carry out their decisions is inescapable.

Public workers are thus likely to be of two divergent types. The "macro decision-makers" are more likely to prefer risks and therefore to be more willing to see things changed than will civil servants, the "micro decision-makers and decision-implementers." This difference in tastes can have serious consequences. Drastic changes mandated from the top will be resisted by civil servants interested in avoiding change and its consequent increase in uncertainty. Reforms may never actually take place, even when they are legislated. This dichotomy in effective tastes for change is widened by the tendency of people who view some changes as overwhelmingly important to be especially attracted to the job of politician.

There would seem to be quite a number of other implications of this dichotomy in the tastes of public workers. For example, it may be that society as a whole is more risk averse than politicians are. Such a difference in tastes would also have implications for the desirability of actual social policies. If politicians are likely to desire more change than is socially desirable—and civil servants less—what is the outcome?

Ability and willingness to accept risk varies across socioeconomic groups. The rich, if only because they can afford it, seem to be more likely to take risks of a given size than the poor. The rich are therefore more likely to try for political office, and because of their superior wealth, more likely to succeed. The long-run implications of this may be quite drastic. If people learn by doing, and learn more the more real the doing, then the children of the rich may, for lack of real practice, be relatively poor at choosing among alternatives in a world where resources are scarce, simply because scarcity is not really part of their experience.[10]

C. Power

Acton [1] observed that power tended to corrupt and that absolute power tended to corrupt absolutely. Actually, it is worse than that. *Ceteris paribus,* power is more valuable to someone who is willing to abuse it in his own interests than to someone who is not. Thus, there exists some tendency for precisely the wrong people to be attracted to positions of power. The correctness and importance of this point is rather easily seen in the context of one of the simple examples often used to "prove" that the existence of government is necessary or desirable.

Consider a group of home owners whose homes all front on the same swamp, and suppose that while the total cost of draining the swamp is less than the total benefit, it is greater than the benefit any single home owner will enjoy from the draining. Thus, no single individual is going to drain the swamp, and, to follow the usual story line, voluntary contributions will not work because some people would lie about the value to them of draining the swamp. "Gamers" might even suggest that they liked the swamp and require compensation for allowing it to be drained. But if some people would deceive, others would not, and to whom is the job of tax assessor likely to seem more valuable? *Ceteris paribus,* those who are not willing to pay their fair share must value the job more highly, since it will provide them with an excellent opportunity for avoiding paying their share, while to the others this element has no value, since they wish to pay their share. Similarly, the job of policeman will appear singularly attractive to those with an interest in committing criminal acts, as well as those who have a strong desire to enforce the law.[11]

In addition to attracting those who would wish to abuse it, power will tend to attract those who like to exercise power for its own sake, and repel those who do not. Public officials often betray a striking tendency to prefer coercive as opposed to non-coercive solutions to problems. This follows directly from the nature of the type of individual attracted to that work. In the recent energy squeeze, proposed solutions to the problem—reduce speed limits, ration gas, close stations on weekend, as opposed to allowing the price to rise and providing direct cash (or voucher) subsidies to the poor who drive to work—all provide eloquent support for this conclusion, as well as suggesting the basic undesirability of allowing people with coercive tendencies to have power.

D. Shirking

Finally, because of the size of public organizations, and because of the general absence in them of a residual income recipient, the opportunity for shirking there is likely to be exceptionally large (see Auster [2]). Individuals with high preferences for on-the-job leisure are likely to find public employment singularly attractive and, as a result, one expects that output per man is rather lower in the public sector than in the economy at large. Unfortunately, given the way in which we generally measure the output of a public agency, this is undetectable at the present time.

II. METHODS OF AMELIORATION

The wrong people seem to be attracted to public work— what can be done? There appear to be at least two viable strategies: improve devices for the detection of adverse personal characteristics, e.g., the screening devices already used by some police departments, and/or alter the nature of public work so as to attract a different type of individual.

It is not at all clear to me how much can be done with screening devices in the absence of further advances in the theory and measurement of personality. It is not easy, perhaps even not possible, to discern the nature of an individual accurately when he is aware that this is being attempted and knows what the "test" criteria are. Even lie-detector tests can be cheated on successfully. It is difficult to judge anyone's character in short periods of time, as recent U.S. experience with politicians should have made sufficiently clear. Hope for improvement must lie, it would seem, in the area of altering the nature of public work itself.

In the case of the job of politician, there does seem to be some scope for altering the nature of the job so as to improve the type of characters attracted to the job. With increases in the number of states over time and the growth of population, the sizes of both houses of Congress have increased to the point where an entering member will with almost complete certainty have a negligible influence on the outcomes. This is highly undesirable, but the remedy is obvious: reduce the number of senators to one per state and, similarly, halve the number of congressmen. Besides the obvious reduction in the cost of government which would result, this might increasingly attract the right people to these positions.

Civil service could also be altered so as to improve the type of person attracted to it. There is no reason for job security to be as high as it is in the present civil service system except the desire to avoid the "spoils system." But is it socially desirable to avoid the "spoils system"? To the extent that public agencies are made up and behave independently of the wishes of elected political leaders—one of the effects of civil service—leaders are not viewed as responsible for the outcomes of public policy. This has the effect of removing some of the political leader's incentives to perform his job well, and will, *ceteris paribus,* lower the probability that the job will be performed as well as it should be. In addition, civil service also removes most of the private incentives civil servants have for performing well, because advancement is generally the result not of actual perform-ance, but of passing an exam with high marks.

Even with these two changes, however, a serious problem would remain. As McKean, Tullock [5, 8] and numerous others have pointed out, the existence of government work necessarily creates new externality-producing activities in society to the extent that government workers can substitute their own satisfaction for that of the public at large. We have pointed out that it is precisely the people who most desire to make this substitution who will be most attracted to public work. Now, as is well known, one way of dealing with this problem is to eliminate the externality by causing the appropriate property rights to be defined, or more simply to alter the situation so that the full consequences of the individual's actions reflect back on him. In order for this to be accomplished, the compensation of public agencies must be related to accurate measures of their output. Judges' salaries, for example, could be related to the number of cases handled or the number of decisions reversed, while public health officials could be paid according to measure-ments of the health of the populations they serve (holding, of course, all other determinants of health constant.) [12]

The military in time of war provides another area of ap-plication. Why have a public army? Could we not simply have offered a prize for defending the South Vietnamese or, better yet, a prize for the surrender of the Viet Cong, and left it to privateers to accomplish the task? [13] Students of military history would not find this an absurd suggestion; privateers have been used successfully in the past. [14] In any case, serious research into the development of accurate measures of government output—measures which are not simply inputs—is absolutely essential. In some cases, how-ever, outputs are not readily measurable, although the ultimate consumer should be able to perceive differences, if only unconsciously. In these cases, a movement towards more voluntary methods of payment would seem desirable. At the very least experimentation seems called for.

It must be understood, however, that the measurement of output, by proxies, which is all that is possible with most public works, is subject to its own problems, at least one of which is worth mentioning. All proxy measures of output of necessity have some flaw or other; they cannot perfectly capture the full reality of what is being produced.[15] This would not in and of itself be much of a problem if it were not so possible for individual actions to increase the inaccuracy of the measures. Clearly, however, that is possible. By focusing their efforts on those parts of the job which are more accurately reflected by the proxy measure and neglecting those which are essentially omitted, individuals can cause the measure to be increasingly inaccurate. Moreover, people probably get better at fooling proxies as time passes, because they generally acquire new insights, conscious or otherwise, into alternative ways in which they can advance their own interests. This suggests that proxy measures of output should be periodically revised, raising the ominous questions of who is to do the revision and how are citizens to prevent the reviser and the people who are subject to the proxy measures of output from establishing trade to their own mutual advantage?

III.   AFTERWORDS

It is often stated that anarchy is only desirable in a world composed of perfectly selfless and moral individuals. Yet, we have shown that predictable types of individuals are attracted to public work and that these are, in general, precisely the wrong types for that work. There is an "adverse selection problem" with respect to public workers. Then perhaps government also is only desirable in a world of perfectly selfless and moral individuals, in which case it is unnecessary. Finally, we have only begun the articulation of the public worker problem. The reader who cares for further insights is directed to Professor Galatin's stimulating comments.

NOTES

1. National defense, by armed might or diplomatic means, etc. A discussion of the range of meaning of "public goods" must be deferred. The remarks also apply to workers producing private goods under government direction and to bureaucracies in general.

2. Admittedly, some jobs may have zero levels of some characteristics.

3. The length of the list is unimportant and perhaps indeterminate. The relative importance, quantitatively, of the various factors is, however, an interesting issue.

4. On the other hand, the hiring process may attempt to take account of the possibility that people with characteristics incompatible with the job exist, and may try to screen them out. More will be said on screening in Section II.

5. This work, apparently, relates in part to that of Downs [3] and Niskanen [6], who distinguish various "bureaucratic types"; however, our list is somewhat different and was derived independently of their works. Niskanen's belief that leisure is not an important argument of the individual's utility function is incorrect in our opinion. This belief, although prevalent among many theorists, is entirely unsupported by any evidence, and flies in the face of such evidence as the dramatic decrease in hours worked over the last 70 years, to cite one example.

6. There is also variation in the levels of these characteristics across civil service jobs. The position of policeman has considerable status and power relative to that of garbage collector. An interesting test of the theory presented here would be to see if there was a positive relationship between the way in which various ethnic groups ranked jobs in terms of status and their composition *ceteris paribus* in these jobs.

7. Of course returns which are negligible for others may not be so for those who are relatively satiated with other forms of gratification, e.g., the ultra-rich, who may also like to gamble.

8. Downs' "Statesmen" are presumably such people; his "Zealots" comprise some of the people distinguished in the preceding paragraph.

9. Silver [7] cites the example of the resistance of the Warsaw ghetto as an example of political participation in the face of certainty of defeat, an illustration of patriotism at work.

10. This is especially true for economic scarcity which may not have been part of their experience at all when they were young and their character and capabilities were formed. In some instances parental training may offset this. Finally, note that almost all Americans may be rich enough to spoil their children in this fashion.

11. Recognizing this, some police departments now attempt to discover which of their applicants would commit crimes by administering lie-detector tests, etc. Whether such programs in fact work is probably open to debate. Apparently Chicago used to use them, no longer does, but is considering using them again. Screening is discussed in Section II. Again, patriots who desire to act against "cheaters" may provide an important countergroup.

12. The Chinese used to pay doctors when they were well and stop payment when they were ill. Niskanen's [6] suggestions must also be considered.

13. We might recall that at the time Sonny Barger (leader of the Hells Angels) was ready to go over and see what his boys could do. I suspect that they could have done more than Willy Westmoreland whose *defenders* could only cite his "logistical genius," the fact that he could relax every day by playing an hour or two's tennis and his life-long association with the Boy Scouts.

14. Why not extend this notion to all of government? Given, and this cannot be given as this paper shows, that we must tax, why must we then produce collectively? Could we not tax, measure output well, and put the jobs up to the lowest bidder, with stiff penalties for failure to deliver and no nonsense about overruns? Salaries and long term contracts are not always efficiency promoting.

15. N. Georgescu-Rogen points to the general inability of a number, or vector of numbers, to perfectly represent the qualities of something [4]. There is always a "qualitative residual." We are pointing out that in some circumstances there is a law of the increasing importance of that residual.

REFERENCES

1. Acton. "Essays on Freedom and Power."
2. Auster, R. D. "The GPITPC and Institutional Entropy," *Public Choice* (Fall, 1974), forthcoming.
3. Downs, A. *Inside Bureaucracy* (Boston: Little, Brown, 1967).
4. Georgescu-Roegen, N. "Concepts Numbers and Quality, in *Analytical Economics* (Cambridge, Mass.: Harvard University Press, 1967).
5. McKean, R. N. "Property Rights within Government and Devices to Increase Governmental Efficiency," *Southern Economic Journal* (Oct., 1972): 177–86.

6. Niskanen, W. A. *Bureaucracy and Representative Government* (Chicago, Illinois: Aldine, Atherton, 1971).
7. Silver, M. "Political Revolution and Repression: An Economic Approach," *Public Choice* (Spring, 1974), forthcoming.
8. Tullock, G. "Public Decisions as Public Goods," *Journal of Political Economy* (July/August, 1971): 913-18.

Comments on
"Some Economic Determinants of the Characteristics of Public Workers"

MALCOLM GALATIN*

I want first to criticize Professor Auster's concentration on the desire to achieve the "public good" as a major attraction to individuals who are thinking of becoming politicians. In many cases, it seems to me, the attraction of a political position is not a desire to advance the "public good" but a desire to advance the good of particular groups, lobbies and centers of power. These goods are likely neither to advance the "public good" nor can they be identified with public goods. Thus a politician has his own constituency and seeks to balance his actions with the wishes of his supporters in order to maintain their support. I would not deny that there may be "growth in office" or a will to achieve the "public good," but to emphasize the latter as a major characteristic of individuals who seek the job of politician ignores the reality of constituency politics in the United States as well as in other countries.

But if, for a moment, we accept Professor Auster's premise that the job of politician attracts those who wish to advance the public good, and these individuals are either (a) the patriotic or (b) those with an unusually large sense of their own historical importance (or luck) or (c) those who hold extreme views about the consequences of

---

* Associate Professor of Economics, The City College of the City University of New York.

alternative policies, does it follow that only patriots who "correctly perceive the correct policy" will be valuable, while the (b) and (c) types are "dangerous people to trust with power?" Surely this depends on an appreciation of what the "correct" policy is, and a belief that there is a lack of congruence between the views of the (b) and (c) types with the "correct" policy. The model that Auster seems to have in mind is a set of objective public policies that further the public good. But how these are to be identified is not discussed. I would suggest that patriotism may be the last refuge of a scoundrel, no matter how sure the patriot and his supporters feel they have correctly perceived the correct policy. Only if we have a well-defined social welfare function for objectively ranking the alternative policies, and then a means for associating motives and potential actions of politician types with this social welfare function, can we carry out the type of analysis that Auster is proposing. And we all know the paradoxes and pitfalls along this path of analysis.

Second, I want to say something about Professor Auster's discussion of risk, and the different attitudes of micro and macro decision-makers to change. Micro decision-makers, the bureaucrats, may resist change, not so much because of risk aversion but because of work aversion. Carrying on a government job with a prescribed set of rules and laws becomes easier over time—there is a good deal of learning by doing. Thus a change in rules or laws—the framework for carrying out public work—involves real work in restructuring old tasks and introducing new tasks. This may be more important than the risk element in the avoidance of change, especially with a tenured civil service. (Parenthetically I should add that politicians may be in a better position to take risks than micro decision-makers, rather than that they are less risk averse in terms of the standard theory. This may be due to differences in wealth and career prospects of politicians compared with bureaucrats, and the fact that bureaucrats have many bets in their portfolios compared with the relatively few that bureaucrats have.)

But even with these remarks, I agree with Professor Auster that the politician is more likely to advocate change than the micro decision-maker—the bureaucrat. However, is this necessarily all bad? The bureaucracy may act as a hindrance and impediment to change advocated by the politician, but these changes may not be correct in terms of correct appreciation of what would be "good" public policy (assuming that we could make this appreciation). This may be due to a number of reasons: in particular, the change advocated by the politician may be to the benefit of his "friends" only, or the advocated change may be based on an incorrect evaluation of the situation, due to the relative lack of information possessed by the politician compared with the information possessed by the "expert" bureaucrat.

Thus, a conservative body of micro decision-makers may act as an important counterweight to a politician by tending to reduce the effects of incorrect public policy. I also agree that because of work/risk aversion the micro decision-makers may also hinder change to a better public policy. But since we have no definition of these "policies," who can say where the balance lies?

Finally, although I do not think that Professor Auster has proved his case that as a generalization the wrong people seem to be attracted to public work, there is no doubt that some wrong people are attracted to some public work. To correct this situation, I agree with his suggestion of improving screening devices, taking full account of the difficulties he mentioned with this approach. The other viable approach, that of altering the nature of public work itself, seems to be the more important, as Professor Auster says. Without necessarily agreeing with his proposed solutions to this problem, there is no doubt that the mea-

surement of output in public work and a better appreciation
of the dividing line between the public and private provision of public goods are vital to the issue.